What Readers Are Saying About
Pragmatic Unit Testing in C#...

"As part of the Mono project, we routinely create and maintain extensive unit tests for our class libraries. This book is a fantastic introduction for those interested in creating solid code."

▶ **Miguel de Icaza,** Mono project, Novell, Inc.

"Andy and Dave have created an excellent, practical, and (of course) very pragmatic guide to unit testing, illustrated with plenty of examples using the latest version of NUnit."

▶ **Charlie Poole,** NUnit framework developer

"Anybody coding in .NET—or, for that matter, any language—would do well to have a copy of this book, not just on their bookshelf but sitting open in front of their monitor. Unit testing is an essential part of any programmer's skill set, and Andy and Dave have written (yet another) essential book on the topic."

▶ **Justin Gehtland,** Founder, Relevance LLC

"The Pragmatic Programmers have done it again with this highly useful guide. Aimed directly at C# programmers using the most popular unit testing package for the language, it goes beyond the basics to show what you should test and how you should test it. Recommended for all .NET developers."

▶ **Mike Gunderloy,**
   Contributing editor, ADT magazine

"Using the approaches described by Dave and Andy, you can reduce greatly the number of defects you put into your code. The result will be faster development of better programs. Try these techniques—they will work for you!"

▶ **Ron Jeffries,** www.XProgramming.com

Pragmatic Unit Testing

in C# with NUnit, Second Edition

Pragmatic Unit Testing
in C# with NUnit, Second Edition

Andy Hunt

Dave Thomas

with Matt Hargett

The Pragmatic Bookshelf
Raleigh, North Carolina   Dallas, Texas

Many of the designations used by manufacturers and sellers to distinguish their products are claimed as trademarks. Where those designations appear in this book, and The Pragmatic Programmers, LLC was aware of a trademark claim, the designations have been printed in initial capital letters or in all capitals. The Pragmatic Starter Kit, The Pragmatic Programmer, Pragmatic Programming, Pragmatic Bookshelf and the linking *"g"* device are trademarks of The Pragmatic Programmers, LLC.

Every precaution was taken in the preparation of this book. However, the publisher assumes no responsibility for errors or omissions, or for damages that may result from the use of information (including program listings) contained herein.

Our Pragmatic courses, workshops and other products can help you and your team create better software and have more fun. For more information, as well as the latest Pragmatic titles, please visit us at:

http://www.pragmaticprogrammer.com

Printed in the United States of America.

ISBN-10: 0-9776166-7-3

ISBN-13: 978-0-9776166-7-1

Printed on acid-free paper with 85% recycled, 30% post-consumer content.

Second printing, December 2009

Version: 2009-12-10

Contents

About the Starter Kit

Our first book, *The Pragmatic Programmer: From Journeyman to Master*, is a widely acclaimed overview of practical topics in modern software development. Since it was first published in 1999, many people have asked us about follow-on books, or sequels. Toward that end, we started our own publishing company, the Pragmatic Bookshelf. By now we have dozens of titles in print and in development and have received major awards and five-star reviews.

But the very first books we published are still some of the most important ones. Before embarking on any sequels to *The Pragmatic Programmer*, we thought we'd go back and offer a prequel of sorts.

Over the years, we've found that many of our pragmatic readers who are just starting out need a helping hand to get their development infrastructure in place so they can begin forming good habits early. Many of our more advanced pragmatic readers understand these topics thoroughly but need help convincing and educating the rest of their team or organization. We think we have got something that can help.

The Pragmatic Starter Kit is a three-volume set that covers the essential basics for modern software development. These volumes include the practices, tools, and philosophies that you need to get a team up and running and productive. Armed with this knowledge, you and your team can adopt good habits easily and enjoy the safety and comfort of a well-established "safety net" for your project.

Volume I, *Pragmatic Version Control*, describes how to use version control as the cornerstone of a project.

A project without version control is like a word processor without an Undo button: the more text you enter, the more expensive a mistake will be. *Pragmatic Version Control* shows you how to use version control systems effectively, with all the benefits and safety but without crippling bureaucracy or lengthy, tedious procedures.

This volume, *Pragmatic Unit Testing*, is the second volume in the series. Unit testing is an essential technique because it provides real-world, real-time feedback for developers as we write code. Many developers misunderstand unit testing and don't realize that it makes our jobs as developers easier. This volume is available in two different language versions: in Java with JUnit and in C# with NUnit.

Volume III, *Pragmatic Automation*, covers the essential practices and technologies needed to automate your code's build, test, and release procedures. Few projects suffer from having too much time on their hands, so *Pragmatic Automation* will show you how to get the computer to do more of the mundane tasks by itself, freeing you to concentrate on the more interesting—and difficult—challenges.

These books were created in the same approachable style as our first book, and they address specific needs and problems that you face in the trenches every day. But these aren't dummy-level books that give you only part of the picture; they'll give you enough understanding that you'll be able to invent your own solutions to the novel problems you face that we *haven't* addressed specifically.

For up-to-date information on these and other books, as well as related pragmatic resources for developers and managers, please visit us on the Web at the following address:

```
http://www.pragmaticprogrammer.com
```

Thanks, and remember to make it fun!

Preface

Welcome to the world of developer-centric unit testing! We hope you find this book to be a valuable resource for you and your project team. You can tell us how it helped you—or let us know how we can improve—by visiting the *Pragmatic Unit Testing* page on our website[1] and clicking Feedback.

Feedback is what makes books great. It's also what makes people and projects great. Pragmatic programming is all about using real-world feedback to fine-tune and adjust your approach.

And that brings us to unit testing. As we'll see, unit testing is important to us as programmers because it provides the feedback we need. Without unit testing, we may as well be writing programs on yellow legal pads and hoping for the best when they're run.

That's not very pragmatic.

This book can help. It is aimed primarily at the C# programmer who has some experience writing and designing code but who does not have much experience with unit testing.

Although the examples are in C#, using the NUnit framework, the concepts remain the same whether you are writing in C++, Fortran, Ruby, Smalltalk, or Visual Basic. Testing frameworks similar to NUnit exist for more than 60 languages; you can download these various frameworks for free.[2]

---

[1]http://www.pragmaticprogrammer.com/titles/utc2
[2]http://www.xprogramming.com/software.htm

For the more advanced programmer who has done unit testing before, we hope there will be a couple of nice surprises for you here. Skim the basics of using NUnit, and concentrate on how to think about tests, how testing affects design, and how to handle certain team-wide issues you may be having.

And remember that this book is just the beginning. It may be your first book on unit testing, but we hope it won't be your last.

Where to Find the Code

Throughout the book you'll find examples of C# code; some of these are complete programs, while others are fragments of programs. If you want to run any of the example code or look at the complete source (instead of just the printed fragment), look in the margin: the filename of each code fragment in the book is printed in the margin next to the code fragment itself.

Some code fragments evolve with the discussion, so you may find the same source code file (with the same name) in the main directory as well as in subdirectories that contain later versions (rev1, rev2, and so on).

All the code in this book is available via the *Pragmatic Unit Testing* page on our website.

Typographic Conventions

The following are the conventions we used in this book:

italic font	Italic font indicates terms that are being defined or borrowed from another language.
`computer font`	This font indicates method names, file and class names, and various other literal strings.
`xxx xx xx;`	This indicates unimportant portions of source code that are deliberately omitted.

The "curves ahead" sign warns that this material is more advanced and can safely be skipped on your first reading.

 Joe the Developer, our cartoon friend, sometimes asks a related question that you may find useful.

 This indicates a break in the text where you should stop and think about what has been asked or try an experiment live on a computer before continuing.

Language-Specific Versions

As of this printing, *Pragmatic Unit Testing* is available in two programming language–specific versions:

- In Java with JUnit
- In C# with NUnit

Acknowledgments from the First Edition

We'd especially like to thank the following Practitioners for their valuable input, suggestions, and stories: Mitch Amiano, Nascif Abousalh-Neto, Andrew C. Oliver, Jared Richardson, and Bobby Woolf.

Thanks also to our reviewers who took the time and energy to point out our errors, omissions, and occasionally twisted writing: Gareth Hayter, Dominique Plante, Charlie Poole, Maik Schmidt, and David Starnes.

Matt's Acknowledgments

I want to first thank my amazing husband, Geoff Huang, for all his patience and support while writing the book and contributing to various related open source projects. Second, gratitude to all the people who have been great pairs to program with and illuminated so much: Bryan Siepert, Rob Myers of NetObjectives, Mike Muldoon, Strick, Anthony

Lineberry, Richard Blaylock, Andre Fonseca, Keith Dreibelbis, Luis Miras, Todd Nagengast, Mike Seery, Cullen Bryan, Katya Androchina, Edward Hieatt, Aaron Peckham, Li Moore, Marcel Prasetya, and Aaron Bawcom. I also want to thank my mom for programming with me as a boy, helping type in very long BASIC programs from various books and magazines.

Last, thanks to Andy Hunt and Robbie Allen for being great editors to work with.

One last-minute tip that didn't quite fit into the book: Don't start a significant house remodel and do a major book project while working a full-time job at the same time.

Andy's Acknowledgments

Thanks to all of you for your hard work and support. A special thank you goes to Matt Hargett for his contributions to this edition and to Steve Peter for the typesetting and layout work.

And thanks to our early reviewers, Cory Foy, Wes Reisz, and Frédérick Ros.

Andy Hunt
July 2007
pragprog@pragmaticprogrammer.com

Chapter 1

Introduction

Lots of different kinds of testing can and should be performed on a software project. Some of this testing requires extensive involvement from the end users; other forms may require teams of dedicated quality assurance personnel or other expensive resources.

But that's not what we're going to talk about here.

Instead, we're going to talk about *unit testing*: an essential, if often misunderstood, part of project and personal success. Unit testing is a relatively inexpensive, easy way to produce better code faster.

Unit testing is the practice of using small bits of code to exercise the code you've written. In this book, we'll be using the NUnit testing framework to help manage and run these little bits of code.

Many organizations have grand intentions when it comes to testing, but they tend to test only toward the end of a project, and then the mounting schedule pressures often cause testing to be curtailed or eliminated entirely.

Everyone agrees that more testing is needed, in the same way that everyone agrees you should eat your broccoli, stop smoking, get plenty of rest, and exercise regularly. That doesn't mean that any of us actually do these things, however.

In fact, many programmers even think testing is a nuisance—an unwanted bother that merely distracts from the real business at hand, which is cutting code.

But unit testing can be much more than a nuisance—although you might consider it to be in the broccoli family, we're here to tell you it's more like an awesome sauce that makes everything taste better. Unit testing isn't designed to achieve some corporate quality initiative; it's not a tool for the end users, managers, or team leads. Unit testing is done by programmers, for programmers. It's here for our benefit alone and can make our lives easier.

Put simply, unit testing can mean the difference between your success and your failure. Consider the following short story.

1.1 Coding with Confidence

Once upon a time—maybe it was last Tuesday—there were two developers, Pat and Dale. They were both up against the same deadline, which was rapidly approaching. Pat was pumping out code pretty fast... developing class after class and method after method and stopping every so often to make sure that the code would compile.

Pat kept up this pace right until the night before the deadline, when it would be time to demonstrate all this code. Pat ran the top-level program but didn't get any output at all. Nothing. It was time to step through using the debugger. Hmm. That can't be right, thought Pat. There's no *way* that this variable could be zero by now. So, Pat stepped back through the code, trying to track down the history of this elusive problem.

It was getting late now. Pat found and fixed the bug, but Pat found several more during the process. And still, there was no output at all. Pat couldn't understand why. It just didn't make any sense.

Dale, meanwhile, wasn't churning out code nearly as fast. Dale would write a new routine and a short test to go along with it. It was nothing fancy... just a simple test to see whether the routine just written actually did what it was supposed to do. It took a little longer to think of the test and write it, but Dale refused to move on until the new routine could prove itself. Only then would Dale move up and write the next routine that called it, and so on.

Dale rarely used the debugger, if ever, and was somewhat puzzled at the picture of Pat, head in hands, muttering various evil-sounding curses at the computer with wide, bloodshot eyes staring at all those debugger windows.

The deadline came and went, and Pat didn't make it. Dale's code was integrated with the other components and ran almost perfectly.[1] One little glitch came up, but it was pretty easy to see where the problem was. Dale fixed the bug in just a few minutes.

Now comes the punch line: Dale and Pat are the same age and have roughly the same coding skills and mental prowess. The only difference is that Dale believes strongly in unit testing and tests every newly crafted method before relying on it or using it from other code. Pat does not. Pat "knows" that the code should work as written and doesn't bother to try it until most of the code has been completed. But by then it's too late, and it becomes very hard to try to locate the source of bugs or even determine what's working and what's not.

1.2   What Is Unit Testing?

A *unit test* is a piece of code written by a developer who exercises a very small, specific area of functionality in the code being tested. Usually a unit test exercises some particular method in a particular context. For example, we might add a large value to a sorted list and then confirm this value appears at the end of the list. Or we might delete a pattern of characters from a string and then confirm that they are gone.

Unit tests are performed to prove that a piece of code does what the developer thinks it should do.

The question remains open as to whether that's the right thing to do according to the customer or end user; that's what acceptance testing is for. We're not really concerned with formal validation and verification or correctness just yet. We're really not even interested in performance testing at this point. All we

---

[1]Thanks to the fact Dale had been continuously integrating via the unit tests all along.

want to do is prove that code does what we intended,[2] so we want to test very small, very isolated pieces of functionality. By building up confidence that the individual pieces work as expected, we can then proceed to assemble and test working systems.

After all, if we aren't sure the code is doing what we think, then any other forms of testing may just be a waste of time. We still need other forms of testing and perhaps much more formal testing depending on our environment. But testing, as with charity, begins at home.

1.3 Why Should We Bother with Unit Testing?

Unit testing will make our lives easier.

Please say that with us, out loud. Unit testing will make our lives easier. That's why we're here. It will make our designs better and drastically reduce the amount of time we spend debugging. We like to write code, and time wasted on debugging is time spent not writing code.

In our earlier tale, Pat got into trouble by assuming that lower-level code worked and then using that in higher-level code, which was in turn used by more code, and so on. Without legitimate confidence in any of the code, Pat was building a "house of cards" of assumptions—one little nudge at the bottom, and the whole thing falls down.

When basic, low-level code isn't reliable, the requisite fixes don't stay at the low level. We fix the low-level problem, but that impacts code at higher levels, which then needs fixing, and so on. Fixes begin to ripple throughout the code, getting larger and more complicated as they go. The house of cards falls down, taking the project with it.

Pat keeps saying things like "That's impossible" or "I don't understand how that could happen." If we find ourselves thinking these sorts of thoughts, then it's usually a good indication that we don't have enough confidence in our code—we don't know for sure what's working and what's not.

---

[2]You also need to ensure you're intending the right thing; see [SH06].

To gain the kind of code confidence that Dale has, you'll need to ask the code itself what it is doing and check that the result is what we expect it to be. Dale's confidence doesn't come from the fact he knows the code forward and backward at all times; it comes from the fact that he has a safety net of tests that verify things work the way he thought they should.

That simple idea describes the heart of unit testing—the single most effective technique to better coding.

1.4   What Do We Want to Accomplish?

It's easy to get carried away with unit testing because the confidence it instills makes coding so much fun, but at the end of the day we still need to produce production code for customers and end users, so let's be clear about our goals for unit testing. We want to do this to make our lives—and the lives of your teammates—easier.

And of course, executable documentation in the form of clearly written unit test code has the benefit of being self-verifiably correct without much effort beyond writing it the first time. Unlike traditional paper-based documentation, it won't drift away from the code (unless, of course, we stop running the tests or let them continuously fail).

Does It Do What We Want?

Fundamentally, we want to answer this question: "Is the code fulfilling our intent?" The code might well be doing the wrong thing as far as the requirements are concerned, but that's a separate exercise. We want the code to prove to us that it's doing exactly what *we* think it should.

Does It Do What We Want All of the Time?

Many developers who claim they do testing only ever write one test. That's the test that goes right down the middle, taking the one well-known "happy path" through the code where everything goes perfectly.

But of course, life is rarely that cooperative, and things don't always go perfectly: exceptions get thrown, disks get full, network lines drop, buffers overflow, and—heaven forbid—we write bugs. That's the "engineering" part of software development. Civil engineers must consider the load on bridges, the effects of high winds, the effects of earthquakes, the effects of floods, and so on. Electrical engineers plan on frequency drift, voltage spikes, noise, and even problems with parts availability.

We don't test a bridge by driving a single car over it right down the middle lane on a clear, calm day. That's not sufficient, and the fact we succeeded is just a coincidence.[3] Beyond ensuring that the code does what we want, we need to ensure that the code does what we want *all of the time*, even when the winds are high, the parameters are suspect, the disk is full, and the network is sluggish.

Can We Depend on It?

Code that we can't depend on is not particularly useful. Worse, code that we *think* we can depend on (but turns out to have bugs) can cost us a lot of time to track down and debug. Few projects can afford to waste time, so we want to avoid that "one step forward, two steps back" approach at all costs and instead stick to moving forward.

No one writes perfect code, and that's OK—as long as we know where the problems exist. Many of the most spectacular software failures that strand broken spacecraft on distant planets or blow them up in midflight could have been avoided simply by knowing the limitations of the software. For instance, the Arianne 5 rocket software reused a library from an older rocket that simply couldn't handle the larger numbers of the higher-flying new rocket.[4] It exploded 40 seconds into flight, taking 500 million dollars with it into oblivion.

---

[3]See *Programming by Coincidence* in [HT00].

[4]For aviation geeks: The numeric overflow was because of a much larger "horizontal bias," which was in turn because of a different trajectory that increased the horizontal velocity of the rocket.

We want to be able to depend on the code we write and know for certain both its strengths and its limitations.

For example, suppose we've written a routine to reverse a list of numbers. As part of testing, we give it an empty list—and the code blows up. The requirements don't say we have to accept an empty list, so maybe we simply document that in the comment block for the method and throw an exception if the routine is called with an empty list. Now we know the limitations of code right away, instead of finding out the hard way (often somewhere inconvenient, such as in the upper atmosphere).

Does It Document Our Intent?

One nice side effect of unit testing is that it helps us communicate the code's intended use. In effect, a unit test behaves as executable documentation, showing how we expect the code to behave under the various conditions we've considered.

Current and future team members can look at the tests for examples of how to use our code. If someone comes across a test case we haven't considered, we'll be alerted quickly to that fact.

1.5 How Do We Do Unit Testing?

Unit testing is basically an easy practice to adopt; we can follow some guidelines and common steps to make it easier and more effective.

The first step is to decide how to test the method in question—before writing the code itself. With at least a rough idea of how to proceed, we can then write the test code itself, either before or concurrently with the implementation code. If we're writing unit tests for existing code, that's fine too, but we may find we need to refactor[5] it more often than with new code in order to make things testable.

---

[5]Refactoring is the process of making small, deterministic changes to the code to reduce coupling and eliminate duplication, without changing the behavior of the code [FBB+99].

\\//
 ? ⌣ **Joe Asks. . .**
 ~
          What's Collateral Damage?

Collateral damage is what happens when a new feature or a bug fix in one part of the system causes a
bug (damage) to another, possibly unrelated part of
the system. It's an insidious problem that, if allowed to
continue, can quickly render the entire system broken
beyond anyone's ability to easily fix.

We sometimes call this the "Whac-a-Mole effect." In
the carnival game of Whac-a-Mole, the player must
strike the mechanical mole heads that pop up on the
playing field. But they don't keep their heads up for
long; as soon as you move to strike one mole, it re-
treats, and another mole pops up on the opposite
side of the field. The moles pop up and down fast
enough that it can be very frustrating to try to con-
nect with one and score. As a result, players generally flail helplessly at the field as the moles continue to
pop up where you least expect them.

Widespread collateral damage to a code base can
have a similar effect. The root of the problem is usually
some kind of inappropriate coupling, coming in forms
such as global state via static variables or false singletons, circular object or class dependencies, and so
on. Eliminate them early to avoid implicit dependencies on this abhorrent practice in other parts of the
code.

Next, we run the test itself and probably all the other tests
in that part of the system, or even the entire system's tests if
that can be done relatively quickly. It's important that *all the
tests pass*, not just the new one. This kind of basic *regression
testing* helps us avoid any collateral damage as well as any
immediate, local bugs.

Every test needs to determine whether it passed—it doesn't
count if you or some other hapless human has to read
through a pile of output and decide whether the code worked.
If you can eyeball it, you can use a code assertion to test it.

You want to get into the habit of looking at the test results and telling at a glance whether it all worked. We'll talk more about that when we go over the specifics of using unit testing frameworks.

1.6 Excuses for Not Testing

Despite our rational and impassioned pleas, some developers will still nod their heads and agree with the need for unit testing but will steadfastly assure us that *they* couldn't possibly do this sort of testing for one of a variety of reasons. Here are some of the most popular excuses we've heard, along with our rebuttals.

"It takes too much time to write the tests." This is the number-one complaint voiced by most newcomers to unit testing. It's untrue, of course, but to see why, we need to talk about where we spend our time when developing code.

Many people view testing of any sort as something that happens toward the end of a project. And yes, if we wait to begin unit testing until then, it will definitely take longer than it would otherwise. In fact, we may not finish the job until the heat death of the universe itself.

At least it will feel that way. It's like trying to clear a couple of acres of land with a lawn mower. If we start early when there's just a field of grasses, the job is easy. If we wait until later, when the field contains thick, gnarled trees and dense, tangled undergrowth, then the job becomes impossibly difficult by hand—we need bulldozers and lots of heavy equipment.

Instead of waiting until the end, it's far cheaper in the long run to adopt the "pay-as-you-go" model. By writing individual tests with the code itself as we go along, there's no crunch at the end, and we experience fewer overall bugs because we are generally always working with tested code. By taking a little extra time all the time, we minimize the risk of needing a huge amount of time at the end.

You see, the trade-off is not "test now" versus "test later." It's linear work now versus exponential work and complexity trying to fix and rework at the end.

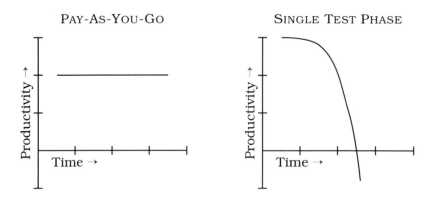

Figure 1.1: COMPARISON OF PAYING-AS-YOU-GO VERSUS HAV-
ING A SINGLE TESTING PHASE

Not only is the job larger and more complex, but now we have
to relearn the code we wrote some weeks or months ago. All
that extra work kills our productivity, as shown in Figure 1.1.
These productivity losses can easily doom a project or developer to being perpetually 90% done.

Notice that testing isn't free. In the pay-as-you-go model,
the effort is not zero; it will cost you some amount of effort
(and time and money). But look at the frightening direction
the curve on the right takes over time—straight down. Our
productivity might even become negative. These productivity
losses can easily doom a project.

So if you think you don't have time to write tests in addition to
the code you're already writing, consider the following ques-
tions:

- How much time do you spend debugging code that you
  or others have written?
- How much time do you spend reworking code that you
  thought was working but turned out to have major, crippling bugs?
- How much time do you spend isolating a reported bug to
  its source?

For most people who work without unit tests, these numbers
add up fast and will continue to add up even faster over the

life span of the project. Proper unit testing can dramatically reduce these times, freeing up enough time so that we'll have the opportunity to write all the unit tests we want—and maybe even some free time to spare.

"It takes too long to run the tests." It shouldn't. Most unit tests should execute in the blink of an eye, so we should be able to run hundreds or even thousands of them in a matter of a few seconds. But sometimes that won't be possible, and we may end up with certain tests that simply take too long to run conveniently all of the time.

In that case, we'll want to separate the longer-running tests from the short ones. NUnit has functionality that handles this nicely, which we'll talk about more later. Run the long tests only in the automated build or manually at the beginning of the day while catching up on email, and run the shorter tests constantly at every significant change or before every commit to the source repository.

"My legacy code is impossible to test." Many people offer the excuse that they can't possibly do unit testing because the existing, legacy code base is such a tangled mess that it's impossible to get into the middle of it and create an individual test. Testing even a small part of the system might mean we have to drag the *entire* system along for the ride, and making any changes is a fragile, risky business.[6]

The problem isn't with unit testing, of course; the problem is with the poorly written legacy code. We'll have to *refactor*— incrementally redesign and adapt—the legacy code to untangle the mess. Note that this doesn't really qualify as making changes just for the sake of testing. The real power of unit tests is the design feedback that, when acted upon appropriately, will lead to better object-oriented designs.

Coding in a culture of fear because we are paralyzed by legacy code is not productive; it's bad for the project, bad for the programmers, and ultimately bad for business. Introducing unit testing helps break that paralysis.

---

[6]See [Fea04] for details on working effectively with legacy code.

"It's not my job to test my code." Now here's an interesting excuse. Pray tell, what *is* our job exactly? Presumably our job, at least in part, is to create working, maintainable code. If we are throwing code over the wall to some testing group without any assurance that it's working, then we're not doing your job. It's not polite to expect others to clean up our own messes, and in extreme cases submitting large volumes of buggy code can become a "career-limiting" move.

On the other hand, if the testers or QA group find it difficult to find fault with our code, our reputation will grow rapidly—along with our job security!

"I don't really know how the code is supposed to behave, so I can't test it." If we truly don't know how the code is supposed to behave, then maybe this isn't the time to be writing it.[7] Maybe a prototype would be more appropriate as a first step to help clarify the requirements.

If we don't know what the code is supposed to do, then how will we know that it does it?

"But it compiles!" OK, no one *really* comes out with this as an excuse, at least not out loud. But it's easy to get lulled into thinking that a successful compile is somehow a mark of approval and that we've passed some threshold of goodness.

But the compiler's blessing is a pretty shallow compliment. It can verify that your syntax is correct, but it can't figure out what your code should do. For example, the C# compiler can easily determine that this line is wrong:

```
statuc void Main() {
```

It's just a simple typo and should be `static`, not `statuc`. That's the easy part. But now suppose we've written the following:

```
public void Addit(Object anObject) {
  List myList = new List();
  myList.Add(anObject);
  myList.Add(anObject);
  // more code...
}
```

Main.cs

---

[7] See [HT00] or [SH06] for more on learning requirements.

Did we really mean to add the same object to the same list twice? Maybe, maybe not. The compiler can't tell the difference; only we know what we intended the code to do.[8]

"I'm being paid to write code, not to write tests." By that same logic, we're not being paid to spend all day in the debugger either. Presumably we are being paid to write *working* code, and unit tests are merely a tool toward that end, in the same fashion as an editor, an IDE, or the compiler.

"I feel guilty about putting testers and QA staff out of work." Don't worry, we won't. Remember we're talking only about *unit testing* here. It's the barest-bones, lowest-level testing that's designed for us, the programmers. There's plenty of other work to be done in the way of functional testing, acceptance testing, performance and environmental testing, validation and verification, formal analysis, and so on.

"My company won't let me run unit tests on the live system." Whoa! We're talking about developer unit testing here. Although you might be able to run those same tests in other contexts (on the live production system, for instance), *they are no longer unit tests.* Run your unit tests on your machine using your own database or using a mock object (see Chapter 6).

If the QA department or other testing staff wants to run these tests in a production or staging environment, you might be able to coordinate the technical details with that department, but realize that they are no longer unit tests in that context.

"Yeah, we unit test already." Unit testing is one of the practices that is typically marked by effusive and consistent enthusiasm. If the team isn't enthusiastic, maybe they aren't doing it right. See whether you recognize any of the following warning signs:

- Unit tests are in fact integration tests, requiring lots of setup and test code, taking a long time to run, and

---

[8]Automated testing tools that generate their own tests based on your existing code fall into this same trap—they can use only what we wrote, not what we meant.

accessing resources such as databases and services on the network.

- Unit tests are scarce and test only one path, don't test for exceptional conditions (no disk space and so on), and don't really express what the code is supposed to do.

- Unit tests are not maintained; tests are ignored (or deleted) forever if they start failing, or no new unit tests are added, even when bugs are encountered that illustrate holes in the coverage of the unit tests.

If you find any of these symptoms, then your team is not unit testing effectively or optimally. Have everyone read up on unit testing again, go to some training, or try pair programming to get a fresh perspective.

1.7 Road Map

Chapter 2, *Your First Unit Tests*, contains an overview of test writing. From there we'll take a look at the specifics of writing tests in NUnit in Chapter 3. We'll then spend a few chapters on how you come up with *what* things need testing and how to test them.

Next we'll look at the important properties of good tests in Chapter 7, followed by what we need to do to use testing effectively in projects in Chapter 8. This chapter also discusses how to handle existing projects with legacy code.

We'll then talk about how testing can influence an application's design (for the better) in Chapter 9, *Design Issues*. We'll then wrap up with an overview of GUI testing in Chapter 10.

The appendixes contain additional useful information: a look at common unit testing problems, extending NUnit itself, a note on installing NUnit, and a list of resources including the bibliography. We finish off with a summary of the book's tips and suggestions.

So, sit back, relax, and welcome to the world of better coding.

## Chapter 2

Your First Unit Tests

As we said in the introduction, a unit test is just a piece of code. It's a piece of code we write that happens to exercise another piece of code and that determines whether the other piece of code is behaving as expected.

How do you do that exactly?

To check whether code is behaving as you expect, you use an *assertion*, a simple method call that verifies something is true. For instance, the method IsTrue checks that the given boolean condition is true and fails the current test if it is not. It might be implemented like the following:

```
public void IsTrue(bool condition)
{
  if (!condition)
  {
    throw new ArgumentException(
      "Expected true", "condition"
    );
  }
}
```

AssertTrue.cs

You could use this assertion method to check all sorts of things, including whether numbers are equal to each other:

```
int actual = 2;



IsTrue(actual == 2);

```

If for some reason `actual` does not equal 2 when the method `IsTrue` is called, then the program will throw an exception.

Since we tend to check for equality a lot, it might be easier to have an assertion method just for numbers. To check that two integers are equal, for instance, you could write a method that takes two integer parameters:

```
public void AreEqual(int actual, int expected)
{
  IsTrue(actual == expected);
}
```

Armed with just these two assertion methods, you can start writing some tests. From here on, we'll generally refer to assertion methods as *asserts* for short. We'll look at more asserts and describe the details of how to use asserts in unit test code in the next chapter. But first, let's consider what tests we might need before writing any code at all.

2.1 Planning Tests

We'll start with a simple example—a single, static method designed to find the largest number in a list of numbers:

```
static int Largest(int[] list);
```

In other words, given an array of numbers such as [7, 8, 9], this method should return 9. That's a reasonable first test. What other tests can you think of off the top of your head? Take a minute to write down as many tests as you can think of for this simple method before you continue reading.

Think about this for a moment before reading on. . .

How many tests did you come up with?

It shouldn't matter what order the given list is in, so right off the bat you've got the following test ideas (which we've written as "what you pass in" → "what you expect").

- [7, 8, 9] → 9
- [8, 9, 7] → 9
- [9, 7, 8] → 9

What happens if there are duplicate largest numbers?

- [7, 9, 8, 9] → 9

Since these are int types, not objects, we probably don't care which 9 is returned, as long as one of them is.

What if there's only one number?

- [1] → 1

And what happens with negative numbers:

- [-9, -8, -7] → -7

It might look odd, but indeed -7 is larger than -9. We're glad we straightened that out now, rather than in the debugger or in production code where it might not be so obvious. This isn't a comprehensive list by any means, but it's good enough to get started with.

We could write our first test and then let that drive our implementation, making sure the implementation passes the tests at each step. Alternately, we could write the implementation and then fill in the tests to see whether what we wrote actually works. To help make all this discussion more concrete, we'll do the latter: write a "largest" method and test it using these unit tests we just described. Here's the code for our first implementation:

```
Line 1   using System;
     -   public class Cmp
     -   {
     5     public static int Largest(int[] list)
     -     {
     -       int index, max=Int32.MaxValue;
     -       for (index = 0; index < list.Length-1; index++)
     -       {
    10         if (list[index] > max)
     -         {
     -           max = list[index];
     -         }
     -       }
    15       return max;
     -     }
     -   }
```

Largest.cs

Now that we've got some ideas for tests, we'll look at writing these tests in C# by using the NUnit framework.

2.2 Testing a Simple Method

Ordinarily we want to make the first test we write incredibly simple, because there is much to be tested the first time besides the code itself: all of that messy business of class names and assembly references, as well as making sure it compiles. We want to get all of that taken care of and out of the way with the very first, simplest test; we won't have to worry about it anymore after that, and we won't have to debug complex integration issues at the same time we're debugging a complex test!

First, let's just test the simple case of passing in a small array with a couple of unique numbers. Here's the complete source code for the test class. We'll explain all about test classes in the next chapter; for now, just concentrate on the assert statements:

```
using System;
using NUnit.Framework;
using NUnit.Framework.SyntaxHelpers;

[TestFixture]
public class LargestTest
{
  [Test]
  public void LargestOf3()
  {
    int[] numbers;
    numbers = new int[] {8, 9, 7};
    Assert.That(Cmp.Largest(numbers), Is.EqualTo(9));
  }
}
```

LargestTest.cs

C# note: The odd-looking syntax to create an anonymous array is just for your authors' benefit because we are lazy and do not like to type. If you prefer, you could write the test this way instead (although the previous syntax is idiomatic):

```
[Test]
public void LargestOf3Alt()
{
  int[] numbers = new int[3];
  numbers[0] = 8;
  numbers[1] = 9;
  numbers[2] = 7;
  Assert.That(Cmp.Largest(numbers), Is.EqualTo(9));
}
```

LargestTest.cs

That's all it takes, and we have our first test.

We want to run this simple test and make sure it passes; to do that, we need to take a quick look at running tests using NUnit.

2.3 Running Tests with NUnit

NUnit is a freely available,[1] open source product that provides a testing framework and test runners. It's available as C# source code that we can compile and install ourselves and as a ZIP file of the binaries. The binaries in the ZIP will run on Microsoft .NET on Windows, and possibly other .NET implementations on Linux/Unix or Mac OS X. There is also an MSI package available, but we recommend just using the ZIP file for the least amount of hassle.

Linux and Mac OS users may want to look at Mono, an open source implementation of the ECMA standards upon which C# and .NET are based. Although Mono ships with its own version of NUnit, we recommend referencing your own copy of NUnit, downloaded separately. This will insulate you from changes to the version of NUnit distributed by the Mono team. We discuss more of these project-oriented details in Chapter 8.

Next, we need to compile the code we've shown. If you're using Visual Studio or SharpDevelop, create a new project for this sample code of type *Class Library*. Type our "production" code into a file named `Largest.cs` and our new test code into a file named `LargestTest.cs`. If you'd rather not type these programs from scratch, you'll be pleased to know that all the source code for this book is available from our website.[2]

Notice that the test code uses `NUnit.Framework`; you'll need to add a reference to `nunit.framework.dll` in order to compile this code. In any of the IDEs mentioned, expand the project's node in the Solution Explorer, open the context menu on the References folder, and then select Add Reference. Once there, browse to the `nunit.framework.dll` from the NUnit install directory.

---

[1] `http://www.nunit.org`
[2] `http://www.pragmaticprogrammer.com/titles/utc2`

 **Joe Asks...**

What's the Deal with Open Source?

What is open source exactly? *Open source software* (OSS) refers to products where the source code is made freely available. Typically this means we can obtain the product for free, and we are also free to modify it, add to it, redistribute it, and so on.

Is it safe to use? For the most part, open source products are safer to use than their commercial, closed-source counterparts, because they are open to examination by thousands of other interested developers. Malicious programs, spyware, viruses, and other similar problems are rare to nonexistent in the open source community.

Is it legal? Absolutely. Just as we are free to write a song or a book and give it away (or sell it), we are free to write code and give it away (or sell it). A variety of open source licenses exist that clarify the freedoms involved. Before you distribute any software that includes open source components, you should carefully check the particular license agreements involved.

Can we contribute? We certainly hope so! The strength of open source comes from people all over the world—people just like you, who know how to program and have a need for some particular feature. Would you like to add a feature to NUnit, SharpDevelop, or Mono? You can! You can edit the source code to the library or one of the test runners and change it and use those changes yourself. You can email your changes to the maintainers of the product, and they may even incorporate your changes into the next release. You can also submit changes using the project's patch tracker or discussion forum; that way, even if your change is not included in an official release, other users can take advantage of it.

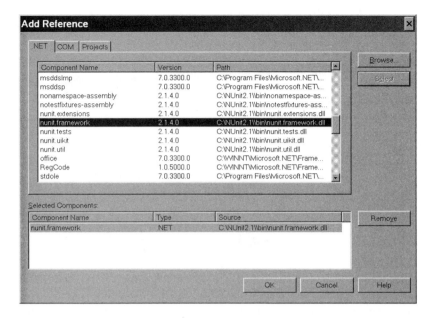

Figure 2.1: ADDING NUNIT ASSEMBLY REFERENCE

Click the Select button to add the DLL to the component list, as shown in Figure 2.1. Click OK, and now your project will be able to use the functionality of the NUnit framework.

Go ahead and build the project as you normally would. (In Visual Studio, pressing Ctrl+Shift+B works well.) Using Mono, we'd invoke the compiler using something such as this:

```
gmcs -debug -t:library -r:System -r:lib/nunit/nunit.framework.dll \
                    -out:Largest.dll Largest.cs LargestTest.cs
```

(The reference to `nunit.framework.dll` will of course be the location where we copied the NUnit distribution.)

Now we've got an assembly. But it's just a library. How can we run it?

Test runners to the rescue! A test runner knows to look for the `[TestFixture]` attribute of a class and for the `[Test]` methods within it. The runner will run the tests, accumulate some statistics on which tests passed and failed, and report the results to you. In this book, we focus on test runners that are easily accessible and freely available.

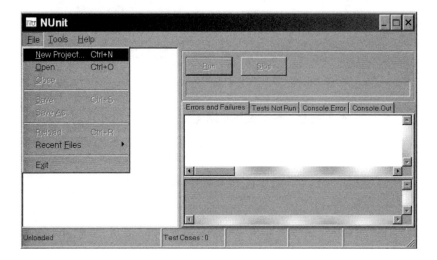

Figure 2.2: CREATING A NEW PROJECT

We can use a test runner in these main ways:

- NUnit GUI (all platforms)

- NUnit command line (all platforms)

- TestDriven.NET (Windows-only)

- SharpDevelop 2.1 runner (Windows-only)

- MonoDevelop 0.13 runner (all platforms)

NUnit GUI

We can start the NUnit GUI in a number of ways: if we unzipped the binaries on Windows, we can just point Windows
Explorer at the directory and double-click `nunit.exe`. If we
unzipped the binaries on Mac OS or Linux, we can run NUnit
GUI via the Mono runtime executable (using `mono -debug
nunit.exe`). If we used the Windows installer, we can use
the shortcuts on our Windows desktop and in the Programs
menu of the Start menu to start the NUnit GUI.

When the GUI comes up, we've got a couple of choices. We
can create a new NUnit project, as shown in Figure 2.2, navi-
gate to the source directory, and create the NUnit project file.

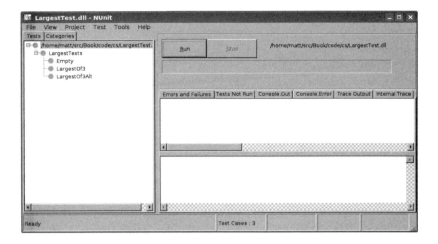

Figure 2.3: NUNIT LOADED AND READY

Then under the Project menu, add assemblies or Visual Studio projects to the NUnit project.[3]

Alternatively, we can just open an assembly (a .dll or .exe file) directly. In Figure 2.3, we've loaded our tests directly from the DLL. It's ready to be tested by either clicking the Run button or pressing Alt+R on the keyboard.

When we run a selected test, the GUI will display a large, colored, status bar. If all the tests pass, the bar is a happy shade of bright green. If any test fails, the bar becomes an angry red. If the bar is a cautionary yellow, that means some tests were skipped (more on that later).

NUnit Command Line

We can also run NUnit from the command line, which comes in handy when automating the project build and test. We'll need to add the NUnit bin directory to your path (that is, the directory path to wherever you installed the NUnit application, plus \bin).

---

[3]Visual Studio support can be enabled using a preference located in Tools/Options.

Figure 2.4: ADDING TO THE WINDOWS SYSTEM PATH

For the current shell, we can set the path variable at the command line, as in the following example on Windows:

```
C:\> set "PATH=%PATH%;C:\Program Files\Nunit V2.4\bin"
```

For more permanent use, go to Control Panel/System/Advanced/Environment Variable, and add NUnit's bin directory to the path variable (see Figure 2.4).

To run from the command line, type the command nunit-console followed by an NUnit project file or an assembly location. You'll see output something like that shown in Figure 2.5 on the facing page.

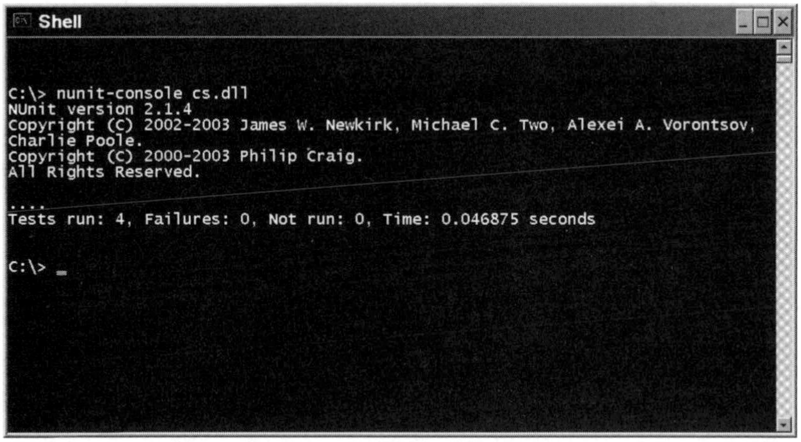

```
Shell                                                    _ □ ×

C:\> nunit-console cs.dll
NUnit version 2.1.4
Copyright (C) 2002-2003 James W. Newkirk, Michael C. Two, Alexei A. Vorontsov,
Charlie Poole.
Copyright (C) 2000-2003 Philip Craig.
All Rights Reserved.

....
Tests run: 4, Failures: 0, Not run: 0, Time: 0.046875 seconds

C:\> _
```

Figure 2.5: NUnit command-line usage

TestDriven.NET (Visual Studio Add-In)

Several add-ins integrate NUnit with Visual Studio. The Test-Driven.NET[4] add-in adds the ability to run or debug any test just by right-clicking the source code and selecting Run Test(s); the output from the tests are reported in Visual Studio's output pane, just like compiler warnings or errors. You can use this output to quickly browse to locations of failed assertions, which is quite handy.

SharpDevelop

SharpDevelop 2.1 (and newer), an open-source IDE written in C#, includes an Eclipse-style integrated test runner. Failed tests come up like compiler errors, allowing for double-clicking an item and going to the assertion that failed. It also allows for measuring the code coverage of unit tests (using NCover[5]) with source code highlighting that can be enabled and disabled. You can see a sample in Figure 2.6 on the next page. See SharpDevelop's web page for more details.[6]

---

[4]http://www.testdriven.net/
[5]NCover is free and can be obtained from http://NCover.org.
[6]http://sharpdevelop.net

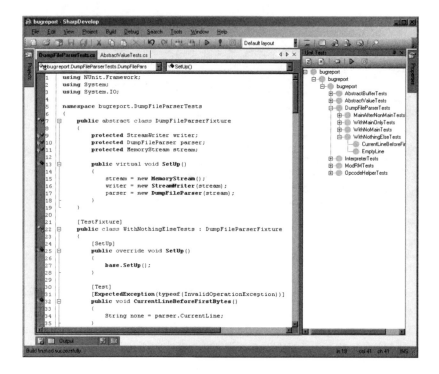

Figure 2.6: SHARPDEVELOP'S INTEGRATED UNIT TESTING

MonoDevelop

MonoDevelop 0.13 and newer, which is based on Sharp-
Develop 0.9, also includes an integrated test runner. Although
not as advanced as SharpDevelop itself, it's a welcome im-
provement over a flat-text editor on platforms where other
tools don't run. For more information, see MonoDevelop's web
page.[7]

2.4   Running the Example

You should be ready to run this first test now.

Try running this example before reading on...

---

[7]http://monodevelop.com

Having just run that code, you probably saw an error similar to the following:

```
Failures:
1) LargestTest.LargestOf3 :
        expected:<9>
          but was:<2147483647>
   at LargestTest.LargestOf3() in c:\LargestTest.cs:line 16
```

Whoops! That didn't go as expected. Why did it return such a huge number instead of our 9? Where could that very large number have come from? It almost looks like the largest number... oh, it's a small typo: `max=Int32.MaxValue` on line 7 should have been `max=0`. We want to initialize `max` so that any other number instantly becomes the next `max`. Let's fix the code, recompile, and run the test again to make sure it works.

Next we'll look at what happens when the largest number appears in different places in the list—first or last, and somewhere in the middle. Bugs most often show up at the "edges." In this case, edges occur when the largest number is at the start or end of the array that we pass in. We can lump all three of these asserts together in one test, but let's add the assert statements one at a time. Notice that just as in production (nontest) code, we have to exercise care, taste, and restraint when deciding how much code to add to one method and when to break that up into multiple methods. Since this method is testing variations on a single theme (physical placement of the largest value), let's put them together in a single method. We already have the case with the largest in the middle:

```
using System;
using NUnit.Framework;
using NUnit.Framework.SyntaxHelpers;
[TestFixture]
public class LargestTest
{
  [Test]
  public void LargestOf3()
  {
    int[] numbers;
    numbers = new int[] {8, 9, 7};
    Assert.That(Cmp.Largest(numbers), Is.EqualTo(9));
  }
}
```

LargestTest.cs

Now try it with the 9 as the first value (we'll just add an assertion to the existing `LargestOf3()` method):

```
[Test]
public void LargestOf3()
{
  int[] numbers;
  numbers = new int[] {9, 8, 7};
  Assert.That(Cmp.Largest(numbers), Is.EqualTo(9));
  numbers = new int[] {8, 9, 7};
  Assert.That(Cmp.Largest(numbers), Is.EqualTo(9));
}
```

We're on a roll. Let's do one more, just for the sake of completeness, and we can move on to more interesting tests:

```
[Test]
public void LargestOf3()
{
  int[] numbers;
  numbers = new int[] {9, 8, 7};
  Assert.That(Cmp.Largest(numbers), Is.EqualTo(9));
  numbers = new int[] {8, 9, 7};
  Assert.That(Cmp.Largest(numbers), Is.EqualTo(9));
  numbers = new int[] {7, 8, 9};
  Assert.That(Cmp.Largest(numbers), Is.EqualTo(9));
}
```

Try running this example before reading on. . .

```
Failures:
1) LargestTest.LargestOf3 :
      expected:<9>
       but was:<8>
  at LargestTest.LargestOf3() in c:\LargestTest.cs:line 18
```

Why did the test get an 8 as the largest number? It's almost as if the code ignored the last entry in the list. Sure enough, it's another simple typo: the `for` loop is terminating too early. This is an example of the infamous "off-by-one" error. Our code has this:

```
for (index = 0; index < list.Length-1; index++) {
```

But it should be one of the following:

```
for (index = 0; index <= list.Length-1; index++) {
for (index = 0; index < list.Length; index++) {
```

The second expression is idiomatic in languages descended from C (including Java and C#), but as you can see, it's prone to off-by-one errors. Make the changes and run the tests again, but consider that this sort of bug is telling you something: it would be better to use an iterator (using the C# foreach statement) here instead. That way we could avoid this kind of off-by-one error in the future.

Let's check for duplicate largest values; type this in, and run it (we'll show only the newly added methods from here on):

```
[Test]
public void Dups() {
  Assert.That(Cmp.Largest(new int[] {9,7,9,8}), Is.EqualTo(9));
}
```
LargestTest.cs

So far, so good. Now the test for just a single integer:

```
[Test]
public void One() {
    Assert.That(Cmp.Largest(new int[] {1}), Is.EqualTo(1));
}
```
LargestTest.cs

Hey, it worked! We're on a roll now; surely all the bugs we planted in this example have been exorcised by now. Just one more check with negative values:

```
[Test]
public void Negative() {
  int[] negatives = new int[] {-9, -8, -7};
  Assert.That(Cmp.Largest(negatives), Is.EqualTo(-7));
}
```
LargestTest.cs

Try running this example before reading on...

```
Failures:
1) LargestTest.Negative :
        expected:<-7>
          but was:<0>
   at LargestTest.Negative() in c:\LargestTest.cs:line 4
```

Whoops! Where did zero come from?

Looks like choosing 0 to initialize max was a bad idea; what we really wanted was MinValue, so as to be less than all negative numbers as well:

```
max = Int32.MinValue
```

Make that change, and try it again—all the existing tests should continue to pass, including this one now. Unfortunately, the initial specification for the method "largest" is incomplete, because it doesn't say what should happen if the array is empty.

Let's say that it's an error and add some code at the top of the method that will throw a runtime exception if the list length is zero:

```
public static int Largest(int[] list) {
  int index, max=Int32.MinValue;
  if (list.Length == 0) {
    throw new ArgumentException("largest: Empty list");
  }
  // ...
```

Notice that just by thinking of the tests, we've already realized we need a design change. That's not at all unusual and in fact is something we want to capitalize on. So for the last test, we need to check that an exception is thrown when passing in an empty array. We'll talk about testing exceptions in depth on page 56, but for now just trust us:

```
[Test]
[ExpectedException(typeof(ArgumentException))]
public void Empty()
{
  Cmp.Largest(new int[] {});
}
```

Finally, a reminder: all code—test or production—should be clear and simple. Test code *especially* must be easy to understand, even at the expense of performance or verbosity.

2.5 More Tests

We started with a simple method and came up with a couple of interesting tests that actually found some bugs. Note that we didn't go overboard and blindly try every possible number combination; we picked the interesting cases that might expose problems. But are these all the tests you can think of for this method?

What other tests might be appropriate?

Since we'll need to think up tests all of the time, maybe we need a way to think about code that will help us come up with good tests regularly and reliably. We'll talk about that after the next chapter, but first, let's take a more in-depth look at using NUnit.

## Chapter 3

Writing Tests in NUnit

We looked at writing tests somewhat informally in the previous chapter, but now it's time to take a deeper look at the difference between test code and production code, all the various forms of NUnit's code and production code, all the various forms of NUnit's assertions, the structure and composition of NUnit tests, and so on.

3.1 Structuring Unit Tests

Suppose we have a method named CreateAccount; the method encapsulates behavior, and it's behavior that we want to test. Our first test method might be named something like CreateSimpleAccount. The method CreateSimpleAccount will call CreateAccount with the necessary parameters and verify that CreateAccount works as advertised. We can, of course, have many test methods that exercise CreateAccount (not all accounts are simple, after all). Tests should be organized around *behaviors*, not necessarily individual methods.

Figure 3.1 on the next page shows the relationship between these two pieces of code.

The test code is for our internal use only; customers or end users will generally never see it or use it. The production code—that is, the code that will eventually be shipped to a customer and put into production—must not know anything

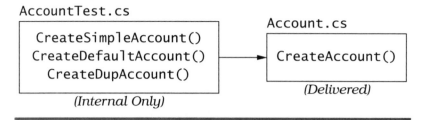

Figure 3.1: TEST CODE AND PRODUCTION CODE

about the test code. Production code will be thrust out into the cold world all alone, without the test code. This typically means that test code is placed under a different project, in its own assembly.

Test code follows a standard formula:

1. Set up all conditions needed for testing (create any required objects, allocate any needed resources, and so on).

2. Call the method to be tested.

3. Verify that the tested functionality worked as expected.

4. Clean up after itself.[1]

We write test code and compile it in the normal fashion, as we would any other bit of source code in our project. It might happen to use some additional libraries, but otherwise there's no magic—it's just code.

When it's time to execute the code, remember that we never actually run the production code directly, at least not the way a user would. Instead, we run the test code, which in turn exercises the production code under very carefully controlled conditions.

Now, although we *could* write all our tests from the ground up, that's not terribly efficient. For the rest of this book we'll assume you're using the NUnit framework. More specifically,

---

[1]This doesn't mean nulling out fields or using GC.Collect(). If you find yourself doing either, you may have a race condition due to a misbehaving finalizer. These issues are almost never limited to test code.

we'll be showing the specific method calls and classes for NUnit 2.4, using C#, in our examples. Earlier or later versions may have slight differences from the details presented here, but the general concepts are the same across all versions and indeed for any testing framework in any language or environment.

3.2 Classic Asserts

As we've seen, some helper methods can assist us in determining whether a method under test is performing correctly. Generically, we call all these helper methods *assertions* (or *asserts* for short). They let us assert that some condition is true, that two bits of data are equal or not, and so on. NUnit 2.4 introduced a new constraint style of assertions while still supporting the classic style of assertions that more closely matches other XUnit frameworks. We'll start by covering some basic classic-style assertions before diving into the constraint-style assertions.

All of the following methods will report failures (that's when the assertion is false) or errors (that's when we get an unexpected exception) and report these through the NUnit test runner. For the text version of the test runner, that means the details of the failure will be printed to the console. The GUI versions of the test runner will show a red bar and supporting details to indicate a failure. We can also output the test results to an XML file.

When a failure or error occurs, execution of the current test method is aborted. Other tests within the same test fixture will still be run.

Asserts are the fundamental building block for unit tests; the NUnit library provides a number of different forms of assertions as static methods in the `Assert` class. Here are a few of those built-in asserts.

AreEqual

```
Assert.AreEqual(expected, actual [, string message])
```

This is the most often used form of assert. *expected* is a value we hope to see (typically hard-coded), and *actual* is a value actually produced by the code under test. *message* is an optional message that will be reported in the event of a failure. We recommend omitting the *message* string. It's better that the name of the namespace, class, and test method itself expresses our intent. We use the appropriate `Assert` method, or we split the test into two methods to keep it focused and the method names unambiguous. We'll show examples of all these practices in a bit.

Any kind of object can be tested for equality; the appropriate `Equals` method will be used for the comparison.[2] In particular, we can compare the contents of strings using this method. Different method signatures are also provided for all the native types (`int`, `float`, and so on) and `Object`. Some objects require deeper inspection to determine equality, such as String, Array, and Collection objects. These object types have their own classic-style asserter classes with extra methods, `StringAssert` and `CollectionAssert`, which we'll get into a bit later.

Computers cannot represent all floating-point numbers exactly and will usually be off a little bit. Because of this, if we are using an assert to compare floating-point numbers (floats or doubles in C#), we need to specify one additional piece of information, the tolerance. This specifies just how close to "equals" we need the result to be:

```
Assert.AreEqual(expected,
                actual,
                tolerance [, string message])
```

For business applications, four or five decimal places is probably enough. For scientific applications, we may need greater precision.

As an example, the following assert will check that the actual result is equal to 3.33 but look only at the first two decimal places:

---

[2]Remember that the default `Equals()` inherited from `System.Object` checks to see only whether the object references themselves are the same—it checks for identity rather than equality. For value types (structs, enums, and so on), the fields are verified to be equal [Ric06].

```
Assert.AreEqual(3.33, 10.0/3.0, 0.01);
```

Less/Greater

```
Assert.Less(x, y)
Assert.Greater(x, y)
```

This asserts that x < y (or x > y) for numeric types or any type that is IComparable.

LessOrEqual/GreaterOrEqual

```
Assert.LessOrEqual(x, y)
Assert.GreaterOrEqual(x, y)
```

This asserts that x <= y (or x >= y) for numeric types, types that overload the <= or >= operators, or any type that implements the IComparable interface.

IsNull/IsNotNull

```
Assert.IsNull(object [, string message])
Assert.IsNotNull(object [, string message])
```

This asserts that the given object is null (or not null), failing otherwise. The message is optional.

AreSame

```
Assert.AreSame(expected, actual [, string message])
```

This asserts that *expected* and *actual* refer to the same object and fails the test if they do not. The message is optional.

IsTrue

```
Assert.IsTrue(bool condition [, string message])
```

This asserts that the given boolean condition is true; otherwise, the test fails. The message is optional.

If we find test code that is littered with the following, then we should be concerned:

```
Assert.IsTrue(true);
```

Unless that construct is used to verify some sort of branching or exception logic, it's probably a bad idea. In particular, what we really don't want to see is a whole page of "test" code with a single `Assert.IsTrue(true)` at the very end (that is, "the code made it to the very end without blowing up; therefore, it must work"). That's not testing; that's wishful thinking.

In addition to testing for `true`, we can also test for `false`:

```
Assert.IsFalse(bool condition [, string message])
```

This asserts that the given boolean condition is false; otherwise, the test fails. The message is optional.

Neither `IsTrue` nor `IsFalse` give us any additional information when the test fails; this means we might have to use the debugger or `Console.WriteLine()` statements to diagnose a unit test failure. That's not very efficient.

There might be a better assertion we could use, such as `StringAssert.Contains()` or `CollectionAssert.DoesNotContain()`—we'll take a look at these more interesting assertions in just a moment. A more precise assertion like those will give us more precise information on failure so we can concentrate on fixing the code rather than trying to figure out what went wrong.

Fail

```
Assert.Fail([string message])
```

This fails the test immediately, with the optional message. `Assert.Fail` can be used to mark sections of test code that should not be reached but isn't really used much in practice.

3.3 Constraint-Based Asserts

NUnit 2.4 introduced a new style of assertions that are a little less procedural and allow for a more object-oriented underlying implementation. NUnit has a history of innovating on the classic XUnit design, which other frameworks then incorporate. In this case, the NUnit team decided to mimic another innovative framework called NMock2,[3] which we'll discuss in Chapter 6.

The term *constraint* describes this new assertion style. Multiple expectations can be evaluated together in a single assertion, *constraining* the test conditions to a single filter. That being said, we don't have to use multiple constraints in a single assertion. Here is a brief example:

```
Assert.That(4, Is.LessThan(5) & Is.GreaterThan(0));
```

This new assertion style can seem a little odd at first, but we suggest giving it a chance before you consider falling back to the "classic" assertion methods. After all, the classic assertion methods just delegate to the constraint-style assertion methods behind the covers. Let's look at a couple of assertions as they would be written in the new style.

Is.EqualTo

```
Assert.That(actual, Is.EqualTo(expected))
```

This is equivalent to the `Assert.AreEqual()` classic assertion method we discussed in the previous section. The `Is.EqualTo()` method is a syntax helper in the `NUnit.Framework.SyntaxHelpers` namespace. It's a static method that just returns an `EqualConstraint` object. The following code is equivalent but may not read as smoothly to some folks:

```
Assert.That(actual, new EqualConstraint(expected))
```

To specify a tolerance for floating-point numbers like we did previously, we can use a neat feature of the new syntax called *constraint modifiers*. There are several that we'll look at, but here is one called `Within()` that is equivalent to the same example that used the classic style in the previous section:

```
Assert.That(10.0/3.0, Is.EqualTo(3.33).Within(0.01f));
```

Is.Not.EqualTo

```
Assert.That(actual, Is.Not.EqualTo(expected))
```

---

[3]NMock2, in turn, was mimicking jMock.

Joe Asks...
What Was Wrong with the Old Syntax?

Nothing was particularly wrong with the classic syntax per se. In fact, there are no plans to remove or deprecate the classic syntax. The classic-style assert methods delegate to the new constraint-style methods, so there's no duplication. Here's a quick history lesson that may illuminate the progression.[a]

In the beginning, test fixture classes had to derive from a class called `TestCase`. Deriving from `TestCase` both told the test runner which classes contained test methods and provided assertion methods, amongst other things. The `TestCase` class was a bit overloaded as far as its responsibilities.

NUnit introduced attributes to mark test fixture classes and extracted the growing list of assertion methods into the family of `Assert` classes. This effectively eliminated the `TestCase` class altogether.

While developing NUnit 2.4, the NUnit team realized that the `Assert` classes had a few too many responsibilities. The `Assert` classes had to make sure the actual value matched the expected value and formatted the data to be output by the test runner when the assertion failed.

These responsibilities were broken up, with the `Constraint` objects (returned by syntax helpers such as `Is.EqualTo()`) bearing the responsibility of making sure the actual value met the context-specific constraint of the expected value. Constraints are encapsulated in separate objects, meaning multiple constraints can be combined and applied to a single value. That leaves the text formatting when an assertion fails, which falls to the `TextMessageWriter` object that NUnit uses internally.

In short, don't panic. The classic-style assertions won't be euthanized and made into soylent green anytime soon. Give the constraint-style assertions a spin; you might like them.

---

[a]See http://nunit.com/blogs/ for even more details.

This is an example of one of the fun things that the constraint-based syntax allows for and is equivalent to the `Assert.AreNotEqual()` classic assertion that was discussed previously.

The usage of `Not` in this context isn't exactly a separate method, as in the other examples. By applying `Not`, it wraps the `EqualConstraint` in a `NotConstraint` object. The following code is equivalent:

```
Assert.That(
  actual,
  new NotConstraint(new EqualConstraint(expected))
);
```

We can apply `Not` to any `Is` or `Has` syntax helper. As such, we could also wrap the `NotConstraint` object around any other `Constraint` object. However, that's rather verbose, so we're probably better off using the syntax helper approach.

Is.AtMost

```
Assert.That(actual, Is.AtMost(expected))
```

This constraint-style assert is equivalent to the `Assert.LessOrEqual()` classic assertion method. `Is.AtMost()` is just an alias for `Is.LessThanOrEqualTo()`, which returns a `LessThanOrEqualConstraint` object.

Is.Null

```
Assert.That(expected, Is.Null);
```

This asserts that *expected* is `null` and fails the test if it is not. To assert the opposite, we have two choices of constraint-style syntax:

```
Assert.That(expected, Is.Not.Null);
```

```
Assert.That(expected, !Is.Null);
```

Either of these ways will wrap the constraint in a `NotConstraint` object under the covers. Either style can be applied to any of the constraints.

Is.Empty

```
Assert.That(expected, Is.Empty);
```

This asserts that *expected* is an empty collection or string and fails the test if it is not.

Is.AtLeast

```
Assert.That(actual, Is.AtLeast(expected));
```

This is equivalent to `Is.GreaterThanOrEqualTo()`, which asserts that *actual* $>=$ *expected* (or *expected* $<=$ *actual*) for numeric types or any type that is `IComparable`.

Is.InstanceOfType

```
Assert.That(actual, Is.InstanceOfType(expected));
```

This asserts that *actual* is of type *expected* or a derivation of that type.

Has.Length

```
Assert.That(actual, Has.Length(expected));
```

This asserts that *actual* has a `Length` property that returns the expected value. Note that it can be any object with a property named "Length," not just a `string` or `Collection`. We could also just assert the length using `Is.EqualTo()`, but this may be easier to read for some.

In the rest of the examples, we'll be using this new constraint style of assertions. If you're more comfortable with the classic style, feel free to substitute those into the appropriate places instead.

Using Asserts

We usually have multiple asserts in a given test method as we prove various aspects and relationships of the method(s) under test. When an assert fails, that test method will be aborted—the remaining assertions in that method will not be executed this time. But that shouldn't be of any concern; we have to fix the failing test before we can proceed anyway. And we fix the next failing test. And the next. And so on.

We should normally expect that all tests pass all of the time. In practice, that means when we introduce a bug, only one or two tests fail. Isolating the problem is usually pretty easy in that environment.

Under *no* circumstances should we continue to add features when there are failing tests! Fix any test as soon as it fails, and keep *all* tests passing *all* of the time.

To maintain that discipline, we'll need an easy way to run all the tests—or to run groups of tests, particular subsystems, and so on.

3.4 NUnit Framework

So far, we've just looked at the assert methods themselves. But we can't just stick assert methods in a source file and expect it to work; we need a little bit more of a framework than that. Fortunately, it's not too much more.

Here is a simple piece of test code that illustrates the minimum framework we need to get started:

```
Line 1    using System;
          using NUnit.Framework;
          using NUnit.Framework.SyntaxHelpers;

      5   [TestFixture]
          public class LargestTest
          {
            [Test]
            public void LargestOf3Alt()
     10     {
              int[] numbers = new int[3];
              numbers[0] = 8;
              numbers[1] = 9;
              numbers[2] = 7;
     15       Assert.That(Cmp.Largest(numbers), Is.EqualTo(9));
            }
          }
```
LargestTest.cs

This code is pretty straightforward, but let's take a look at each part in turn.

 **Joe Asks...**

What's a Fixture?

From the c2.com wiki:[a]

In electronics testing, a fixture is an environment in which we can test a component. Once the circuit board or component is mounted in the test fixture, it is provided with the power and whatever else is needed to drive the behavior to be tested. Negative testing in this scenario can include providing power inputs beyond the normally expected range or raising the environmental temperature to ensure the component continues to operate under out-of-spec conditions.

A fixture in the context of unit testing is more about the scenario we're testing than the actual class we're testing. Testing a single class across multiple fixtures is common.

[a]http://c2.com/cgi/wiki?TestFixture

First, the `using` statement on line 2 brings in the necessary NUnit classes. Remember, we'll need to tell the compiler to reference `nunit.framework.dll`; otherwise, the `using` statement won't be able to find the `NUnit.Framework` namespace.

Next, we have the class definition itself on line 6: each class that contains tests must be annotated with a [`TestFixture`] attribute as shown. The class must be declared `public` (so that the test runners will run it; by default, classes are `internal`), and it must have a public, no-parameter constructor (the default implicit constructor is all we need—adding a constructor to a `TestFixture` is generally not necessary).

Finally, the test class contains individual methods annotated with [`Test`] attributes. In the example, we've got one test method named `LargestOf3` on line 10. Any public, parameterless method specified with a [`Test`] attribute will be run automatically by NUnit. We can include helper methods to support clean code in our tests as well; we just don't mark them as tests.

In the previous example, we showed a single test, using a single assert, in a single test method. Of course, inside a test method, we can place any number of asserts:

```
using System;
using NUnit.Framework;
using NUnit.Framework.SyntaxHelpers;
[TestFixture]
public class LargestTest
{
  [Test]
  public void LargestOf3()
  {
    int[] numbers;
    numbers = new int[] {9, 8, 7};
    Assert.That(Cmp.Largest(numbers), Is.EqualTo(9));
    numbers = new int[] {8, 9, 7};
    Assert.That(Cmp.Largest(numbers), Is.EqualTo(9));
    numbers = new int[] {7, 8, 9};
    Assert.That(Cmp.Largest(numbers), Is.EqualTo(9));
  }
```

LargestTest.cs

Here we have three calls to `Assert.That` inside a single test method.

3.5 NUnit Test Selection

As we've seen so far, a fixture (that is, a class marked with the [TestFixture] attribute) contains test methods; each test method contains one or more assertions. Multiple test fixtures can be included in a source code file or a compiled assembly.

We will ordinarily run all the tests within an assembly just by specifying the assembly to the test runner. We can also choose to run individual test fixtures within an assembly using either the NUnit command line or the GUI.

From the GUI, we can select an individual test, a single test fixture, or the entire assembly by selecting it and clicking the Run button, and all the appropriate tests will be run.

From the command line, we can specify the assembly and a particular test fixture as follows:

```
c:\> nunit-console assemblyname.dll /fixture:ClassName
```

Organizing Fixtures

Following good object-oriented design, a class should be focused on one responsibility. This applies to test fixtures as well—they're just classes, after all. As such, put tests into a fixture whose name describes the specific scenario in which they are being tested. This is an important concept. Test fixtures should be focused on verifying behavior in a specific scenario.

If there aren't multiple scenarios, then just name the fixture class after the class being tested. We can always extract more focused fixtures from a general fixture once the general fixture starts getting too fat.

As with any code, if we notice that a certain word or phrase recurs in the names of our fields or methods, this can be a clue that we need to extract those methods to a new class. To eliminate this subtle form of duplication, extract a fixture class focused on a specific scenario, with a name that documents that scenario.

To keep things readable in the test runner output, favor putting fixture classes under a namespace that includes the name of the class that the fixtures are testing, like so:

```
namespace ZeroBay.Test.ShoppingCartTest
{
  [TestFixture]
  public class EmptyCartFixture
  {
    [Test]
    public void OverallRateIsZero() {...}
  }
}
```

Given this flexibility, we may want to think a bit about how to organize test methods into individual assemblies and fixtures to make testing easier.

For instance, we may want to run all the database-related tests at once or all the tests that Fred wrote (Fred is still on probation from the last project, and we want to keep an eye on him).

Fortunately, NUnit has a mechanism we can use to categorize and classify individual test methods and fixtures.

Categories

NUnit provides an easy way to mark and run individual tests and fixtures by using *categories*. A category is just a name that we define. We can associate different test methods with one or more categories, and then we can select which categories we want to exclude (or include) when running the tests.

Suppose among our tests we've got a method to find the shortest route that our traveling salesman, Bob, can take to visit the top n cities in his territory. The funny thing about the traveling salesman algorithm is that for a small number of cities it works just fine, but it's an *exponential* algorithm.

That means that a few hundred cities might take 20,000 years to run, for example. Even 50 cities takes a few hours, so we probably don't want to include that test by default.

We can use NUnit categories to help sort out our usual tests that we can run constantly versus long-running tests that we'd rather run only during the automated build. To this end, categories are generally used for exclusion rather than inclusion.

A category is specified as an attribute. We provide a string to identify the category when we declare the method. Then when we run the tests, we can specify which categories we want to run (we can specify more than one).

For instance, suppose we've got a few methods that take only a few seconds to run but one method that takes a long time to run.

We can annotate them using the category names "Short" and "Long" (we might also consider making a category "Fred" if we still want to keep an eye on him):

```
Line 1    using NUnit.Framework;
    -     using NUnit.Framework.SyntaxHelpers;
    -
    -     [TestFixture]
    5     public class ShortestPathTest
    -     {
    -       TSP tsp;
    -
    -       [SetUp]
    10      public void SetUp()
    -       {
    -         tsp = new TSP();
    -       }
    -
    15      [Test]
    -       [Category("Short")]
    -       public void Use5Cities()
    -       {
    -         Assert.That(tsp.ShortestPath(5), Is.AtMost(140));
    20      }
    -
    -       // This one takes a while...
    -       [Test]
    -       [Category("Long")]
    25      [Category("Fred")]
    -       public void Use50Cities()
    -       {
    -         Assert.That(tsp.ShortestPath(50), Is.AtMost(2300));
    -       }
    30    }
```

Notice that we can specify multiple attributes (in this case, Test and Category) on two separate lines, as shown around line 26, or combined into one line.

Now if we choose to run just "Short" methods, the method Use5Cities will be selected to run. If we choose "Long" methods, only Use50Cities will be selected. We can also select both categories to run all these methods.

In the GUI, we select which categories of tests to include and which to exclude on the tab, as shown in Figure 3.2 on the facing page. Just select each category you're interested in, and click the Add button.

On a real project, of course, we wouldn't bother to mark a bunch of tests as "Short." They should *all* be short, except for the ones specifically marked as "Long."

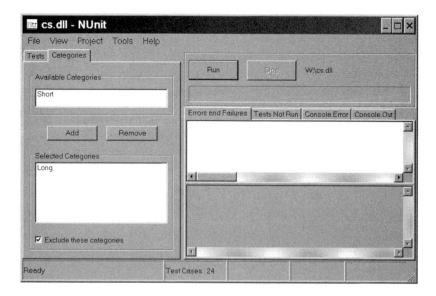

Figure 3.2: NUNIT CATEGORY SELECTION

This is why categories are generally used for exclusion—we want most of our tests to run by default, without the error-prone annoyance of manually including them.

We can *exclude* the listed categories so all other tests except those in the named categories run. There's a check box in the GUI for this; the command line option is, conveniently enough, /exclude. Just add the following parameter to the command line:

```
/exclude=category1;category2;...
```

Note that multiple category names are separated by a semi-colon (;).

From the command line, we can specify individual categories to include as well, with the /include parameter. In the GUI, add categories to the list, but don't check the box to exclude the categories.

But this isn't quite enough: it turns out that although some categories of tests should be run when no categories are selected, others should run only when explicitly selected.

To support this, we can specify the `Explicit` attribute:

```
[Explicit("SpecialEquipmentNeeded")]
```

This syntax automatically excludes the category from any run that doesn't specify any categories.

By default, our run will include tests without categories and tests with nonexplicit categories. However, if even one category is specified in the GUI or on the command line, then only that single category will be run.

There's a danger here, of course—these tests aren't running all the time. They probably aren't being run in the automated build system either. This might lull you into a false sense of security, so beware.

In addition to marking individual test methods as belonging to a category, we can also mark entire fixtures. For instance, if we wanted to flag our entire test fixture as long-running (without having to mark each and every test method), we could do so.

```
Line 1   using NUnit.Framework;
    -    using NUnit.Framework.SyntaxHelpers;
    -
    -    [TestFixture]
    5    [Category("Long")]
    -    public class ShortestPathTest-Revised
    -    {
    -      TSP tsp;
    -
   10      [Test]
    -      public void Use50Cities()
    -      {
    -        tsp = new TSP(); // load with default cities
    -        Assert.That(tsp.ShortestPath(50), Is.AtMost(2300));
   15      }
    -
    -      [Test]
    -      public void Use100Cities()
    -      {
   20        tsp = new TSP(); // load with default cities
    -        Assert.That(tsp.ShortestPath(100), Is.AtMost(4675));
    -      }
    -
    -      [Test]
   25      public void Use150Cities()
    -      {
    -        tsp = new TSP(); // load with default cities
    -        Assert.That(tsp.ShortestPath(150), Is.AtMost(5357));
    -      }
   30    }
```

Now we can quickly exclude the whole fixture by using a category name.

Of course, not all tests need categories, and we may have entire projects where there are no categories at all. But it's nice to know they are there if we do need them.

Per-Method Setup and Teardown

Each test should run independently of every other test; this allows us to run any individual test at any time, in any order.

To accomplish this feat, we may need to reset some parts of the testing environment in between tests or clean up after a test has run. NUnit lets us specify two methods to set up and then tear down the environment per test using attributes:

```
[SetUp]
public void PerTestSetup()
{
  ...
}
[TearDown]
public void PerTestTeardown()
{
  ...
}
```

In this example, the method `PerTestSetup()` is called before each one of the [Test] methods is executed, and the method `PerTestTeardown()` is called after each test method is executed, even if the test method throws an exception. This is why we mentioned that constructors in test fixtures generally aren't necessary. Constructors wouldn't work the way we wanted them to anyway, since NUnit doesn't necessarily re-create the `TestFixture` class each time it runs a test; it discovers and runs these methods using reflection.

Per-Fixture Setup and Teardown

Normally per-method setup is all we need, but in some circumstances we may need to set something up or clean up after the *entire* test class has run; for that, we need per-fixture setup and teardown (the difference between per-test and per-fixture execution order is shown in Figure 3.3 on the next page).

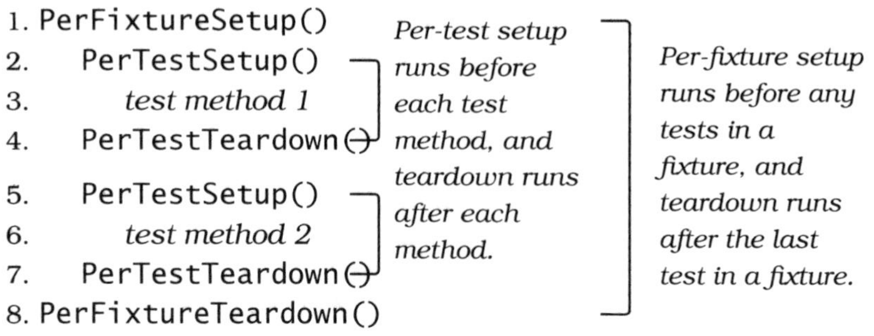

1. PerFixtureSetup()
2.   PerTestSetup()
3.   test method 1
4.   PerTestTeardown()
5.   PerTestSetup()
6.   test method 2
7.   PerTestTeardown()
8. PerFixtureTeardown()

Per-test setup runs before each test method, and teardown runs after each method.

Per-fixture setup runs before any tests in a fixture, and teardown runs after the last test in a fixture.

Figure 3.3: EXECUTION ORDER OF SETUP CODE

All we need to do is annotate our setup methods with the following attributes:

```
[TestFixtureSetUp]
public void PerFixtureSetup()
{
  ...
}
[TestFixtureTearDown]
public void PerFixtureTeardown()
{
  ...
}
```

For example, suppose we needed some sort of database connection object for each test. Rather than duplicating code in each test method that connects to and disconnects from the database, we could simply use SetUp and TearDown methods. Since creating the initial connection to the database can be slow, we may want to do that only once before all the tests run by using TestFixtureSetUp.

```
[TestFixture]
public class DBTest
{
  private Connection dbConn;
  [TestFixtureSetUp]
  public void PerFixtureSetup()
  {
    dbConn = new Connection("mysql", 1521, "user", "pw");
    dbConn.Connect();
  }
```

```
[SetUp]
public void PerTestSetup()
{
  // populate database with test data
}
[TearDown]
public void PerTestTearDown()
{
  // clean up database to avoid pollution
}
[TestFixtureTearDown]
public void PerFixtureTeardown()
{
  dbConn.Disconnect();
  dbConn.Dispose();
}
[Test]
public void AccountAccess()
{
  // Uses dbConn
  xxx. xxx xxxxxx xxx xxxxxxxx;
  xx xxx xxx xxxx x xx xxxxx;
}
[Test]
public void EmployeeAccess()
{
  // Uses dbConn
  xxx. xxx xxxxxx xxx xxxxxxxx;
  xxxx x x xx xxx xx xxxx;
}
}
```

DBTest.cs

In this example, the method PerFixtureSetup will be called before the method PerTestSetup, which in turn will be called before AccountAccess. After AccountAccess has finished, PerTestTearDown will be called, followed by PerFixture-TearDown. PerFixtureSetup will be called again, followed by PerTestSetup again, then EmployeeAccess, and then Per-TestTeardown, followed by PerFixtureTearDown again.

Note that we can use both per-fixture and per-test methods in the same class. Although setup and teardown methods generally come in pairs, they don't have to do so. Often, a fixture will have a setup but no teardown. A teardown without a setup, although rare, is also not unheard of. It can happen when the initialization of an object that implements IDisposable is different for every test method, but we always want to call the Dispose method on the object in the teardown method.

We can also define setup methods across inheritance boundaries, in both base classes and derived classes. NUnit will correctly stitch together all of the annotated methods. We'll talk about this more later.

Implementing a Simple Fixture

Now that you've learned about how `SetUp` and `TearDown` methods work, try creating a new test fixture class that uses all of them. In the `SetUp` method, put a `Console.WriteLine` that outputs something like `"SetUp called"`. Put similar code in for the other methods we just discussed. Add a couple of test methods as well; the `SetUp` and `TearDown` methods for a fixture will be run only if a test is actually present. If you're using `nunit-console` to run the test, you'll see your output mixed in with the test runner's console output. If you're using the NUnit GUI, you'll see your output on the tab labeled Console.Out. All of the IDEs mentioned previously have an "output" pad where you can view this information.

Try running this example before reading on...

Note that leaving console I/O in real test code is usually not something we recommend. If you prefer adding "tombstones"[4] for debugging rather than using a debugger, you're not alone; just don't leave the console I/O in the tests.

3.6 More NUnit Asserts

In addition to the basic asserts we've discussed, NUnit provides asserts to aid in testing collections and files. If you prefer the classic-style assertion methods, check out the `StringAssert` and `CollectionAssert` classes as well as the NUnit documentation.

---

[4]In this context, tombstones are used figuratively to describe things we trip over when running through code that is dead or dying.

List.Contains

```
Assert.That(actualCollection,
            List.Contains(expectedValue))
Assert.That({5, 3, 2}, List.Contains(2))
```

This tests that the expected value is contained within actualCollection.

Is.SubsetOf

```
Assert.That(actualCollection,
            Is.SubsetOf(expectedCollection))
Assert.That(new byte[] {5, 3, 2},
            Is.SubsetOf(new byte[] {1, 2, 3, 4, 5}))
```

This tests that the elements of actualCollection are contained within expectedCollection, regardless of order.

Text.StartsWith

```
Assert.That(actual,
            Text.StartsWith(expected))
Assert.That("header:data.",
            Text.StartsWith("header:"))
```

This tests that the expected string is at the beginning of actual. This is case sensitive by default; to ignore case sensitivity, we need to add the IgnoreCase constraint modifier:

```
Assert.That("header:data.",
            Text.StartsWith("HeadeR:").IgnoreCase)
```

Text.Matches

```
Assert.That(actual, Text.Matches(expected))
Assert.That("header:data.",
            Text.Matches(@"header.*\."))
```

This tests that the expected regular expression string matches actual. Here we're making sure the actual string starts with *header* and ends with a period character. We could also have used a combination of Text.StartsWith, Text.EndsWith, or Text.Contains constraints.

FileAssert.AreEqual/AreNotEqual

```
FileAssert.AreEqual(FileInfo expected,
            FileInfo actual)
FileAssert.AreEqual(String pathToExpected,
            String pathToActual)
```

These test whether two files are the same, byte for byte. Note that if we do the work of opening a `Stream` (file-based or not), we can use the `EqualsConstraint` instead, like so:

```
Stream expectedStream = File.OpenRead("expected.bin");
Stream actualStream = File.OpenRead("actual.bin");
Assert.That(
  actualStream,
  Is.EqualTo(expectedStream)
);
```

3.7 NUnit Custom Asserts

The standard asserts that NUnit provides are usually sufficient for most testing. However, we may run into a situation where it would be handy to have our own, customized asserts. Perhaps we've got a special data type or a common sequence of actions that is done in multiple tests.

The worst thing we can do is slavishly copy the same sequence of test code over and over again. "Copy and paste" of common code in the tests can be a fatal disease.

Instead, tests should be written to the same high standards as regular code, which means honoring good coding practices such as the DRY principle,[5] loose coupling, orthogonality, and so on. Factor out common bits of test harness into real methods, and use those methods in your test cases.

This is real code, and it needs to be well-written and well-factored so we can reuse it and keep it up-to-date easily as the system grows and evolves.

Don't be afraid to write your own assertion-style methods. For instance, suppose we are testing a financial application and virtually all the tests use a data type called `Money`:

---

[5]DRY stands for "Don't Repeat Yourself." It's a fundamental technique that demands that every piece of knowledge in a system must have a single, unambiguous, and authoritative representation [HT00].

```
using System;
using NUnit.Framework;
using NUnit.Framework.SyntaxHelpers;
public class MoneyAssert
{
  // Assert that the amount of money is an even
  // number of dollars (no cents)
  public static void AssertNoCents(Money amount,
                                   String message)
  {
    Assert.That(
        Decimal.Truncate(amount.AsDecimal()),
        Is.EqualTo(amount.AsDecimal()),
        message);
  }
  // Assert that the amount of money is an even
  // number of dollars (no cents)
  public static void AssertNoCents(Money amount)
  {
    AssertNoCents(amount, String.Empty);
  }
}
```

MoneyAssert.cs

Note that we provide both forms of assert: one that takes a `string` and one that does not. Note also that we didn't duplicate any code in doing so; we merely forward the call.

Now any other test classes in the project that need to test Money can use our own custom assertion method. If multiple test fixture classes needed to use our custom assertions or other support methods, we could also extract a common base fixture class. We'll talk more about that in Chapter 8. In the meantime, here's an example of a test that uses our newly minted MoneyAssert class:

```
using NUnit.Framework;

[TestFixture]
public class HistoryTest
{
  [Test]
  public void CountDeMonet()
  {
    Money money = new Money(42.00);
    money.Add(2);
    MoneyAssert.AssertNoCents(money);
  }
}
```

SomethingTest.cs

For more examples, take a look at the NUnit source code itself (perhaps the `StringAssert` code). That's part of the beauty of open source—you can go see the code for yourself and see how the magic is done.

3.8 NUnit and Exceptions

We might be interested in two different kinds of exceptions:

- Expected exceptions resulting from a test

- Unexpected exceptions from something that has gone horribly wrong

Contrary to what you might think, exceptions are really good things—they tell us that something is wrong. Sometimes in a test, we *want* the method under test to throw an exception. Consider a method named `ImportList()`. It's supposed to throw an `ArgumentNullException` if passed a null list.

Guarding against bad data is good defensive programming. If a null parameter is passed in and not used immediately, the eventual `NullReferenceException` becomes a time bomb of sorts. It will go off at an unexpected moment, in some far-away corner of the code. We then get the unenviable task of tracking down the source of the bad data. But by failing quickly, we'll find the root of the problem quickly and much more easily. Some people just like pain, but we don't, so we prefer to decrease our time spent debugging by employing this practice.

With what we've learned so far, we can construct the following test to ensure that the exception is thrown as expected:

```
[Test]
public void NullList()
{
  try
  {
    WhitePages.ImportList(null);
    Assert.Fail("expected an ArgumentNullException");
  }
  catch (ArgumentNullException)
  {
  }
}
```

This test will fail if any exception other than `Argument-NullException` is thrown or if no exception is thrown at all. If no exception is thrown, the `Assert.Fail()` method is called, which fails the test. If an exception other than `Argument-NullException` is thrown, it won't be caught by the `catch` defined, which fails the test. This works, but it's not exactly aesthetically pleasing.

More practically speaking, this style of test just doesn't express our intentions very well and doesn't scale well to more complicated cases. The NUnit user community and authors agreed, so for expected exceptions, NUnit provides the `[ExpectedException]` attribute:

```
[TestFixture]
public class ImportListTest
{
  [Test]
  [ExpectedException(typeof(ArgumentNullException))]
  public void NullList()
  {
    WhitePages.ImportList(null);
    // Shouldn't get to here
  }
}
```

ExceptionTest.cs

This test method is now expected to throw an exception (from the call to `ImportList()`). If it doesn't, the test will fail. If the exact exception specified is thrown as expected, the test passes. If a different exception is thrown (even a superclass of the one specified), the test fails. It might be tempting to expect just the base `Exception` type, but then we'd be skirting around the fact that either our code is nondeterministic, we don't understand it, or both.

We want to be as specific with exceptions in this context as we would be in a `catch()` statement. Otherwise, we'll get tests that pass when a totally different exception is thrown, and we might not know about it until the system starts malfunctioning in the hands of end users.

Note that once the expected exception is thrown, any remaining code in the test method will be skipped. If the `SetUp` method throws an exception before a test method's code executes, the test will always be reported as failing even though the actual test code didn't run.

Furthermore, even if SetUp throws an exception, the Tear-Down method(s) will still be run (if any are declared).

In general, we should test a method for every expected exception, but what about unexpected exceptions? NUnit will take care of those for us. For instance, suppose we are reading a file of test data. Rather than catching the possible I/O exceptions ourselves, just let them propagate out to the test framework:

```
[Test]
public void ParseData()
{
  StreamReader reader = new StreamReader("data.txt");
  xxx xxx xxxxxx xxxxx xxxx;
}
```

Even better, NUnit will report the *entire* stack trace right down to the bug itself, not just to some failed assert, which helps when trying to figure out why a test failed. If we have enabled debugging information during compilation of our assembly under test, it will also give the exact source code line numbers in the stack trace.

When *compiling* under Mono's C# compiler (gmcs) or Microsoft .NET's C# compiler (csc), add -debug+ to the command line. If you're not working at the command line, this can be accomplished by changing the project settings in your IDE.

When *running* under Mono, you'll need to use the -debug option to the Mono runtime executable (mono -debug) for it to actually use that generated debug information.[6]

3.9 Temporarily Ignoring Tests

Ordinarily, we want all tests to pass all of the time. But suppose we've thought up a bunch of tests first, written them, and are now working our way through implementing the code required to pass the tests. What about all those new tests that would fail now?

---

[6]Microsoft .NET doesn't require this; we hope Mono will remove this requirement in a future release.

We can go ahead and write these tests, but we don't want the testing framework to run these tests just yet. NUnit provides the [Ignore] attribute:

```
[Test]
[Ignore("Out of time.  Will Continue Monday. --AH")]
public void Something()
{
    ...
}
```

ExceptionTest.cs

NUnit will report that this method was skipped (and show a yellow bar in the GUI version) so that you won't forget about it later.

In other testing frameworks and languages, we'd have to either name the method differently or comment it out. In any language, the code still has to compile cleanly; if it's not ready for that yet, then we should comment out the offending parts.

It's a good idea to put a meaningful message, and perhaps even your initials, into the Ignore attribute so that the team knows *why* this test isn't running. Are you still working on it? Do you need something from someone else in order to finish? Can someone else finish it up for you (in a geographically diverse team, perhaps)? Don't just ignore it and forget about it; that's a *broken window*.[7]

We also want to avoid at all costs the habit of *ignoring* failing test results. We don't see green until they all work: just the absence of a red bar (or error messages) does not mean success.

Ignoring Platform-Dependent Tests

There is one small exception to that rule; what do we do when certain tests have to be ignored because of the platform on which you are running? This scenario isn't uncommon and can occur if we're writing a cross-platform C# application; some of our tests may run (or pass) only on a specific platform.

---

[7]See [HT00].

This was a problem NUnit itself faced, so they introduced the Platform attribute, which is used like this:

```
[Test]
[Platform(Exclude = "Mono")]
public void RemoveOnEmpty() {
    ...
}
[Test, Platform(Exclude = "Net-1.0,Win95")]
public void EmptyStatusBar() {
    ...
}
```

In this example, the test named RemoveOnEmpty in the previous code won't run on Mono, regardless of the underlying operating system on which Mono is running. The test named EmptyStatusBar in the example won't run on any .NET 1.0 system *or* on any .NET or Mono version running on Windows 95. As you can see, Linux-specific tests that don't work on Solaris, Mac OS, or certain Windows or .NET versions can be marked as such.[8]

When using the Platform attribute, we will still get a green bar in the GUI (not yellow) even in the presence of tests ignored via this attribute. Other than that, it operates similarly to the Ignore attribute.

The point again is that we want to avoid any situation where we begin to ignore failing tests out of habit. Platform ensures that the proper tests are run only in the proper environment.

Now that we've got a good idea of *how* to write tests, it's time to take a closer look at figuring out *what* to test.

---

[8]You can find a comprehensive list of the platforms in the NUnit documentation at http://nunit.org.

Chapter 4

What to Test: The Right BICEP

Now that we know how to test, we need to spend some chapters looking at what to test, or more precisely, the kinds of things that might need testing.

It can be hard to look at a method or a class, try to come up with all the ways it might fail, and anticipate all the bugs that might be lurking in there. With enough experience, you start to get a feel for those things that are "likely to break," and you can effectively concentrate on testing in those areas first. But without a lot of experience, it can be frustrating trying to discover possible failure modes. End users are quite adept at finding our bugs, but that's both embarrassing and damaging to our careers! What we need are some guidelines— some reminders of areas that might be important to test.

By using our Right BICEP, we can strengthen our testing skills:

- **Right**: Are the results **right**?
- **B**: Are all the **b**oundary conditions correct?
- **I**: Can we check **i**nverse relationships?
- **C**: Can we **c**ross-check results using other means?
- **E**: Can we force **e**rror conditions to happen?
- **P**: Are **p**erformance characteristics within bounds?

4.1 Are the Results Right?

Right | BICEP

The first and most obvious area to test is simply to see whether the expected results are right—to validate the results.

It's a good starting point. We've seen simple data validation already: the tests in Chapter 2 that verify that a method returns the largest number from a list.

These are usually the "easy" tests, and many of these sorts of validations may even be specified in the requirements. If they aren't, we'll probably need to ask someone. We need to be able to answer the key question:

> ***If the code ran correctly, how would we know?***

If we cannot answer this question satisfactorily, then writing the code—or the test—may be a complete waste of time. "But wait," you may say, "that doesn't sound very agile! What if the requirements are vague or incomplete? Does that mean we can't write code until all the requirements are firm?"

No, not at all. If the requirements are truly not yet known or complete, we can always invent some as a stake in the ground. They may not be correct from the user's point of view, but we now know what *we* think the code should do, so we can answer the question.

Of course, we'll then arrange for feedback with users to fine-tune our assumptions. The definition of "correct" may change over the lifetime of the code in question, but at any point, we should be able to prove (using automated tests) that the code is doing what we think it ought to do.

Using Data Files

For sets of tests with large amounts of test data, we might want to consider putting the test values or results in a separate data file that the unit test reads in. This doesn't need to be a very complicated exercise—and we don't even need to use XML.[1] Here is a version of `TestLargest` that reads in all the tests from a data file:

---

[1]This is clearly a joke. XML is mandatory on all projects today, isn't it?

```csharp
using NUnit.Framework.SyntaxHelpers;
using System;
using System.IO;
using System.Collections.Generic;
[TestFixture]
public class LargestDataFileTest
{
  private int[] getNumberList(string line)
  {
    string[] tokens = line.Split(null);
    List<int> numberList = new List<int>();
    for (int i=1; i < tokens.Length; i++)
    {
      numberList.Add(Int32.Parse(tokens[i]));
    }
    return numberList.ToArray();
  }
  private int getLargestNumber(string line)
  {
    string[] tokens = line.Split(null);
    string val = tokens[0];
    int expected = Int32.Parse(val);
    return expected;
  }
  private bool hasComment(string line)
  {
    return line.StartsWith("#");
  }
  // Run all the tests in testdata.txt (does not test
  // exception case). We'll get an error if any of the
  // file I/O goes wrong.
  [Test]
  public void FromFile()
  {
    string line;
    // most IDEs output binaries in bin/[Debug,Release]
    StreamReader reader =
        new StreamReader("../../testdata.txt");
    while ((line = reader.ReadLine()) != null)
    {
      if (hasComment(line))
      {
        continue;
      }
      int[] numbersForLine = getNumberList(line);
      int actualLargest = Cmp.Largest(numbersForLine);
      int expectedLargest = getLargestNumber(line);
      Assert.That(actualLargest,
          Is.EqualTo(expectedLargest));
    }
  }
}
```

The data file has a simple format; each line contains a set of numbers. The first number is the expected answer, and the numbers on the rest of the line are the arguments with which to test. We'll allow a number sign (#) for comments so we can put meaningful descriptions and notes in the test file.

The test file can then be as simple as this:

```
#
# Simple tests:
#
9 7 8 9
9 9 8 7
9 9 8 9
#
# Negative number tests:
#
-7 -7 -8 -9
-7 -8 -7 -8
-7 -9 -7 -8
#
# Mixture:
#
7 -9 -7 -8 7 6 4
9 -1 0 9 -7 4
#
# Boundary conditions:
#
1 1
0 0
2147483647 2147483647
-2147483648 -2147483648
```

In this example, we're running only one particular test (using one assert), but we could extend that to run as many different tests on the same data as practical.

For just a handful of tests (as in this example), the separate data file approach is probably not worth the effort or the performance overhead of the file I/O. In cases where we can't justify an external file, C#'s string literals paired with a **Text-Reader** can provide the same benefits described previously without the less palatable aspects:

```
string oneCommentWithTwoSets = @"
# comment line
9 7 8 9
-9 9 8 7
"
```

But say this was a more advanced application, with tens or even hundreds of test cases in this form. Then the file approach becomes a compelling choice.

Be aware that test data, whether it's in a file or in the test code itself, might well be incorrect. In fact, experience suggests that test data is *more likely* to be incorrect than the code we're testing, especially if the data was hand-calculated or obtained from a system we're replacing (where new features may deliberately cause new results). When test data says you're wrong, double- and triple-check that the test data is right before attacking the code. Ask a co-worker to take a look, or just take a break (away from the keyboard); sometimes it's difficult to see the woods through the trees. One reviewer suggested actually having a test that does some assertions against the test data itself, such as the number of test data sets contained in the file.

Something else to think about is that the code as presented in this example does not test any exception cases. How might we implement that? Also notice that we wrote a nontest "helper" method to parse the numbers from the data file. It's perfectly OK—even encouraged—to create support methods and classes as needed. We might even extract these support methods into a `TestFileParser` class if we wanted to share this code across different fixtures or just to unclutter the test class itself.

Do whatever makes it easiest for you to prove that the method is right.

4.2 Boundary Conditions

In the previous "largest number" example, we discovered several boundary conditions: when the largest value was at the end of the array, when the array contained a negative number, when the array was empty, and so on.

Right **B** *ICEP*

Identifying boundary conditions is in fact one of the most valuable parts of unit testing, because this is where most bugs generally live—at the edges. These nether regions of untested code are the source of almost all exploitable security vulnerabilities.

Here are some conditions to think about:

- Totally bogus or inconsistent input values, such as a filename of `"!*W:X\&Gi/w~>g/h#WQ@"`.

- Badly formatted data that is missing delimiters or terminators, such as an email address without a top-level domain (`"fred@foobar."`).[2]

- Empty or missing values (such as 0, 0.0, an empty string, an empty collection, or `null`) or missing in a sequence (such as a missing TCP packet).

- Values far in excess of reasonable expectations, such as a person's age of 10,000 years or a password string with 10,000 characters in it.

- Duplicates in lists that shouldn't have duplicates.

- Ordered lists that aren't, and vice versa. Try handing a presorted list to a sort algorithm, for instance—or even a reverse-sorted list.

- Things that arrive out of order or happen out of expected order, such as trying to print a document before logging in or getting fragmented IP packets out of order, for instance.

For readers familiar with security testing, these are many of the same things that "fuzzing" tools do to try to find exploitable security bugs in applications. By unit testing for these issues up front, you can make sure your code stands up to this kind of abuse.

An easy way to think of possible boundary conditions is to remember the acronym CORRECT. For each of these items, consider whether similar conditions may exist in your method that you want to test and what might happen if these conditions were violated:

- **Conformance:** Does the value conform to an expected format?

---

[2] A popular mail service suffered from an exploitable bug like this involving a missing > in SMTP headers.

- **O**rdering: Is the set of values ordered or unordered as appropriate?

- **R**ange: Is the value within reasonable minimum and maximum values?

- **R**eference: Does the code reference anything external that isn't under direct control of the code itself?

- **E**xistence: Does the value exist (for example, is non-null, non-zero, present in a set, and so on)?

- **C**ardinality: Are there exactly enough values?

- **T**ime (absolute and relative): Is everything happening in order? At the right time? In time?

Because boundary conditions are such an important area to test, we'll examine these in detail in the next chapter (which makes Right BICEP a nested acronym).

4.3 Check Inverse Relationships

Right B $\boxed{I}$ *CEP*

Some methods can be checked by applying their logical inverse. For instance, we might check a method that calculates a square root by squaring the result and testing that it is tolerably close to the original number:

```
[Test]
public void SquareRootUsingInverse()
{
  double x = MyMath.SquareRoot(4.0);
  Assert.That(4.0, Is.EqualTo(x*x).Within(0.0001));
}
```

RootsTest.cs

We might check that some data was successfully inserted into a database and then search for it and delete it. We might transfer money into an account and then transfer the same amount out of the account. Any of these operations apply an "inverse" to see whether we get back to an original state.

But be cautious when you've written both the original routine and its inverse, because some bugs might be masked by a common error in both routines. Where possible, use a different source for the inverse test. In the square root example, we're just using regular multiplication to test our method. For the database search, we'll probably use a vendor-provided delete routine to test our insertion.

4.4 Cross-Check Using Other Means

Right BI⎡C⎤EP

We might also be able to cross-check the results of our method using different means.

Usually there is more than one way to calculate some quantity; we might pick one algorithm over the others because it performs better or has other desirable characteristics. That's the one we'll use in production, but we can use one of the other versions to cross-check our results in the test system. This technique is especially helpful when there's a proven, known way of accomplishing the task that happens to be too slow or too inflexible to use in production code.

We can use that somewhat lesser version to our advantage to check that our new super-spiffy version is producing the same results:[3]

```
[Test]
public void SquareRootUsingStd()
{
    double number = 3880900.0;
    double root1 = MyMath.SquareRoot(number);
    double root2 = Math.Sqrt(number);
    Assert.That(root2, Is.EqualTo(root1).Within(0.0001));
}
```

Another way of looking at this issue is to use different pieces of data from the class itself to make sure they all "add up," or reconcile. That counts as a cross-check as well.

For instance, suppose you were working on a library's database system (that is, a brick-and-mortar library that lends out real books). In this system, the number of copies of a particular book should always balance. That is, the number of copies that are checked out plus the number of copies

RootsTest.cs

---

[3]Some spreadsheet engines (as found in Microsoft Excel) employ similar techniques to check that the models and methods chosen to solve a particular problem are appropriate and that the answers from different applicable methods agree with each other.

sitting on the shelves should always equal the total number of copies in the collection. These are separate pieces of data and may even be reported by objects of different classes, but they still have to agree and therefore can be used to cross-check one another.

As with the inverse checks shown previously, make sure you aren't simply exercising the same underlying code in two different ways—the point of cross-checking is to explicitly use different code to verify the same result.

4.5 Force Error Conditions

In the real world, errors happen. Disks fill up, network lines drop, email goes into a black hole, and programs crash. You should be able to test that your code handles all these real-world problems by forcing errors to occur. *Right BIC* $\boxed{E}$ *P*

That's easy enough to do with invalid parameters and the like, but simulating specific network errors—without unplugging any cables—takes some special techniques. We'll discuss one way to do this using mock objects in Chapter 6 on page 93.

But before we get there, consider what kinds of errors or other environmental constraints you might introduce to test your method. Make a short list before reading further.

Think about this for a moment before reading on...

Here are a few environmental things we've thought of:

- Running out of memory
- Running out of disk space
- Issues with wall-clock time
- Network availability and errors
- Insufficient file or path permissions
- System load
- Limited color palette
- Very high or very low video resolution

These are just general categories; for each of them there may be more subtle issues worth testing. For instance, we might test that the code can handle the case when the network itself goes down, but what about if the network is up and the DNS server is down? Or what about if the network is up but is slowed to a timeout-inducing crawl because of a denial-of-service attack? These things happen, and if our code needs to handle these sort of errors, then we need to test for them. If our code isn't supposed to handle these sorts of errors, we should still write a test that validates that behavior using the `ExpectedException` we previously discussed.

4.6 Performance Characteristics

Right BICE **P**

One area that might prove beneficial to examine is performance characteristics—not performance itself, but trends as input sizes grow, as problems become more complex, and so on.

What we'd like to achieve is a quick regression test of performance characteristics. All too often, we might release one version of the system that works OK, but somehow by the next release it has become dead-dog slow. We don't know why, what change was made or when, who did it, or anything. And the end users are screaming bloody murder.

To avoid that awkward scenario, we might consider some rough tests just to make sure that the performance curve remains stable. For instance, suppose we've written a filter that identifies websites that we want to block (using our new product to view naughty pictures might get us in all sorts of legal trouble, after all).

The code works fine with a few dozen sample sites, but will it work as well with 10,000? 100,000? Let's write a unit test to find out:

```
Line 1   [TestFixture]
    -    public class FilterTest
    -    {
    -        readonly String naughtyUrl =
             "http://www.xxxxxxxxx.com",
    5        Timer timer;
    -        UrlFilter filter;
    -
```

```
        [SetUp]
        public void SetUp()
10      {
            timer = new Timer();
        }

        [Test]
15      public void SmallList()
        {
            filter = new UrlFilter(SMALL_LIST);
            timer.Start();
            filter.Check(naughtyUrl);
20          timer.End();
            Assert.That(timer.ElapsedTime, Is.LessThan(1.0));
        }

        [Test]
25      [Category("Long")]
        public void HugeList()
        {
            filter = new UrlFilter(HUGE_LIST);
            timer.Start();
30          filter.Check(naughtyUrl);
            timer.End();
            Assert.That(timer.ElapsedTime, Is.LessThan(10.0));
        }
    }
```

FilterTest.cs

This gives us some assurance that we're still meeting performance targets. But because this one test takes six to seven seconds to run, we may not want to run it every time. As long as we run it in our automated build at least every couple of days, we'll quickly be alerted to any problems we may introduce while there is still time to fix them.

## Chapter 5

CORRECT
Boundary Conditions

As we said in the previous chapter, boundary conditions are such a vibrant source of bugs that we need a whole chapter to talk about them. Many bugs in code occur around boundary conditions, that is, under conditions where the code's behavior may be different from the normal, day-to-day routine.

For instance, suppose we have a function that takes two integers:

```
public int Calculate(int a, int b)
{
  return a / (a+b);
}
```

Most of the time, this code will return a number just as we expect. But if the sum of a and b happens to equal zero, we will get a `DivideByZeroException` instead of a return value. That is a boundary condition—at the edge of normal expectations. It's a place where things might suddenly go wrong or at least behave differently from what we wanted.

To help us think of tests for boundary conditions, we'll use the acronym CORRECT:

- **C**onformance: Does the value conform to an expected format?

- **O**rdering: Is the set of values ordered or unordered as appropriate?
- **R**ange: Is the value within reasonable minimum and maximum values?
- **R**eference: Does the code reference anything external that isn't under direct control of the code?
- **E**xistence: Does the value exist (for example, is non-null, non-zero, present in a set, and so on)?
- **C**ardinality: Are there exactly enough values?
- **T**ime (absolute and relative): Is everything happening in order? At the right time? In time?

Let's look at each one of these in turn. Remember that for each of these areas, you want to consider data that is passed in as arguments to your method as well as internal data that you maintain inside your method and class.

The underlying question that we want to answer fully is this:

What else *can go wrong?*

Once you think of something that could go wrong, write a test for it. Once that test passes, again ask yourself, "What else can go wrong?" and write another test, and so on.

There's always something else that could go wrong, and these are some of the more productive areas to consider.

5.1 Conformance

$\boxed{\text{C}}$ ORRECT

Many times we expect or produce data that must conform to some specific format. An email address, for instance, isn't just a simple string. We expect that it must be of this form:

```
name@somewhere.com
```

And it may have the possibility of extra dotted parts:

```
firstname.lastname@subdomain.somewhere.com
```

And it may even have oddballs like this one:

```
firstname.lastname%somewhere@subdomain.somewhere.com
```

Suppose we are writing a method that will extract users' names from their email addresses. We'll expect that a user's name is the portion before the @ sign. What will our code do if there *is* no @ sign? Will it work? Throw an exception? What about multiple @ signs or a string of only @ signs? Is this a boundary condition we need to consider?[1]

Validating formatted string data such as email addresses, phone numbers, account numbers, or filenames is usually straightforward, but be aware of internationalization issues: not only could there be issues with the format (many countries don't have states or provinces), but there could be issues with character encoding as well.[2] Will we be getting Unicode data, and if so, will we be able to handle it?

Then there's more complex, structured data to consider. Suppose we are reading report data that contains a header record linked to a number of data records and finally to a trailer record. How many conditions might we have to test?

- What if there's no header, just data and a trailer?
- What if there's no data, just a header and trailer?
- What if there's no trailer, just a header and data?
- What if there's just a trailer?
- What if there's just a header?
- What if there's just data?

Just as with the simpler email address example, we have to consider what will happen if the data does not conform to the structure we think it should. This directly applies to any code that parses file formats or network protocols, avenues by which attacks will come either purposefully or unwittingly. It's best to code defensively and verify the defenses with unit tests, since an attacker will probably end up testing them for us eventually whether we want them to or not. A fun way to think about this is, "How would we attack this function?"

And of course, if we are creating data such as an email address (possibly building it up from different sources), we want to test our result to make sure it conforms to the specification or RFC as well.

---

[1] Email addresses are actually very complicated. A close reading of RFC 822 may surprise you.

[2] Input validation should always be done on model objects, sometimes in addition to the UI validation.

5.2 Ordering

 C **O** RRECT

Another area to consider is the order of data, or the position of one piece of data within a larger collection. For instance, in the Largest() example in the previous chapter, one bug manifested itself depending on whether the largest number we were searching for was at the beginning or end of the list.

That's one aspect of ordering. Any kind of search routine should be tested for conditions where the search target is first or last, because many common bugs can be found that way.

For another aspect of ordering, suppose we are writing a method that is passed a collection containing a restaurant order. We would probably expect that the appetizers will appear first in the order, followed by the salad (and that all-important dressing choice), then the entree, and finally a decadent dessert involving lots of chocolate.

What happens to our code if the dessert is first and the entree is last?

If there's a chance that sort of thing can happen *and* if it's the responsibility of our method to deal with it if it does, then we need to test for this condition and address the problem. Now, it may be that this is not something our method needs to worry about. Perhaps this needs to be addressed at the user input level (see the "Testing Invalid Parameters" section later in this chapter and the chapter on GUI testing on page 177).

Bear in mind that business logic does not belong in the GUI itself—ever. User interface components (graphical or otherwise) should contain code only for the UI, not for anything else.

If you're writing a sort routine, what might happen if the set of data is already ordered? Or worse yet, sorted in precisely reverse order? Ask yourself whether that could cause trouble—whether these are conditions that might be worth testing, too. Then test it anyway, and you may be surprised to find it makes a difference.

If you are supposed to maintain something in order, verify that it is.

For example, if our method is part of the GUI that is sending the dinner order back to the kitchen, we should have a test that verifies that the items are in the correct serving order:

```
[Test]
public void KitchenOrder()
{
  Order order = new Order();
  FoodItem dessert = new Dessert("Chocolate Decadence");
  FoodItem entree  = new Entree("Beef Oscar");
  FoodItem salad   = new Salad("Parmesan Peppercorn");

  // Add out of order
  order.AddFoodItem(dessert);
  order.AddFoodItem(entree);
  order.AddFoodItem(salad);

  // But should come out in serving order
  IEnumerator<FoodItem> itr = order.GetEnumerator();

  Assert.That(salad, Is.EqualTo(itr.Current));
  itr.MoveNext();
  Assert.That(entree, Is.EqualTo(itr.Current));
  itr.MoveNext();
  Assert.That(dessert, Is.EqualTo(itr.Current));
  itr.MoveNext();

  // No more left
  Assert.That(itr.MoveNext(), Is.False);
}
```

KitchenTest.cs

Of course, from a human-factors standpoint, we'd need to modify the code so that it's flexible enough to allow people to eat their ice cream first, if so desired. In this case, we'd need to add a test to prove that our four-year-old nephew's ice cream comes with everyone else's salads, but that Grandma's ice cream comes at the end with the cappuccino.

5.3 Range

Range is a convenient catchall word for the situation where a variable's type allows it to take on a wider range of values than we need—or want. For instance, a person's age is typically represented as an integer, but no one has ever lived to be 200,000 years old, even though that's a perfectly valid integer value. Similarly, there are only 360 degrees in a circle, even though degrees are commonly stored in an integer.

CO[**R**]RECT

In good object-oriented design, we do not use a built-in value type (for example, an `int` or `Int32`) to store a bounded-integer value such as an age or a compass heading:

```csharp
using System;
//
// Compass bearing
//
public class Bearing
{
  protected int bearing; // 0..359
  //
  // Initialize a bearing to a value from 0..359
  //
  public Bearing(int degrees)
  {
    if (degrees < 0 || degrees > 359)
    {
      throw new ArgumentException("out of range",
                                  "degrees");
    }
    bearing = degrees;
  }
  //
  // Return the angle between our bearing and another.
  // May be negative.
  //
  public int AngleBetween(Bearing another)
  {
    return bearing - another.bearing;
  }
}
```

Bearing.cs

Notice that the angle returned is just an `int`—a plain old number, because we are not placing any range restrictions on the result (it may be negative, and so on).

By encapsulating the concept of a bearing within a class, we now have one place in the system that can filter out bad data. We cannot create a `Bearing` object with out-of-range values. Thus, the rest of the system can use `Bearing` objects and be assured that they contain only reasonable values.[3]

Other ranges may not be as straightforward. For instance, suppose we have a class that maintains two sets of *x, y*

---

[3]For types like these, a `struct` might be preferred if you have a deep enough knowledge of the CLR to care [Ric06].

coordinates. These are just integers, with arbitrary values, but the constraint on the range is such that the two points must describe a rectangle with no side greater than 100 units. That is, the allowed range of values for both *x, y* pairs is interdependent.

We'll want a range test for any method that can affect a coordinate to ensure that the resulting range of the *x, y* pairs remains legitimate. For more information on this topic, see "Invariants" in the chapter that starts on page 153.

Since we will likely call this from a number of different tests, it probably makes sense to make a new assert method:

```
public const int MAX_DIST = 100;
static public void AssertPairInRange(Point one,
                                     Point two,
                                     String message)
{
  Assert.That(
    Math.Abs(one.X - two.X),
    Is.AtMost(MAX_DIST),
    message
  );
  Assert.That(
    Math.Abs(one.Y - two.Y),
    Is.AtMost(MAX_DIST),
    message
  );
}
```

PairTest.cs

But the most common ranges we'll want to test probably depend on physical data structure issues, not on application domain constraints. Take a simple example such as a stack class that implements a stack of `Strings` using an array:

```
public class MyStack
{
  public MyStack()
  {
    elements = new string[100];
    nextIndex = 0;
  }
  public String Pop()
  {
    return elements[--nextIndex];
  }
```

```
// Delete n items from the elements en-masse
public void Delete(int n)
{
  nextIndex -= n;
}
public void Push(string element)
{
  elements[nextIndex++] = element;
}
public String Top()
{
  return elements[nextIndex-1];
}
private int nextIndex;
private string[] elements;
}
```

Some potential bugs are lurking here, because there are no checks at all for either an empty stack or a stack overflow. However we manipulate the index variable `nextIndex`, one thing is supposed to be always true: (next_index >= 0 && next_index < stack.Length). We'd like to check to make sure this expression is true.

Both `nextIndex` and `stack` are private variables; we don't want to have to expose them just for the sake of testing. There are several ways around this problem; for now we'll just make a special method in `MyStack` named `CheckInvariant()`:

```
public void CheckInvariant()
{
  if (!(nextIndex >= 0 &&
        nextIndex  < elements.Length))
  {
    throw new InvariantException(
         "nextIndex out of range: "  +  nextIndex +
         " for elements length " + elements.Length);
  }
}
```

Now a test method can call `CheckInvariant()` to ensure that nothing has gone awry inside the guts of the stack class, without having direct access to those same guts.[4]

---

[4]We'd normally use an `InvalidOperationException`, but in this case we want to reinforce the invariant concept by using a custom exception.

```
using NUnit.Framework;
using NUnit.Framework.SyntaxHelpers;
[TestFixture]
public class MyStackTest
{
  [Test]
  public void Empty()
  {
    MyStack stack = new MyStack();
    stack.CheckInvariant();
    stack.Push("sample");
    stack.CheckInvariant();
    // Popping last element ok
    Assert.That(
      stack.Pop(),
      Is.EqualTo("sample")
    );
    stack.CheckInvariant();
    // Delete from empty stack
    stack.Delete(1);
    stack.CheckInvariant();
  }
}
```

MyStackTest.cs

When we run this test, we'll quickly see that we need to add some range checking!

```
TestCase 'MyStackTest.Empty' failed: InvariantException
nextIndex out of range: -1 for stack length 100
        mystack.cs(34,0): at MyStack.CheckInvariant()
        mystacktest.cs(20,0): at MyStackTest.Empty()
```

It's much easier to find and fix this sort of error here in a simple testing environment instead of buried in a real application.

Almost any indexing concept (whether it's a genuine integer index or not) should be extensively tested. Here are a few ideas to get us started:

- `Start` and `End` index have the same value.

- `First` is greater than `Last`.

- `Index` is negative.

- `Index` is greater than allowed.

- `Count` doesn't match actual number of items.

- ...

5.4 Reference

COR **R** *ECT*

What things does our method reference that are outside the scope of the method itself? Any external dependencies? What state does the class have to be in? What other conditions must exist in order for the method to work?

For example, a method in a web application to display a customer's account history might require that the customer is first logged on. The method Pop() for a stack requires a nonempty stack. Shifting the transmission in a car to Park from Drive requires that the car is stopped.

If we have to make assumptions about the state of the class and the state of other objects or the global application, then we need to test our code to make sure that it is well-behaved if those conditions are not met. For example, the code for the microprocessor-controlled transmission might have unit tests that check for that particular condition: the state of the transmission (whether it can shift into Park) depends on the state of the car (is it in motion or stopped?).

```
[Test]
public void JamItIntoPark()
{
  transmission.Shift(DRIVE);
  car.AccelerateTo(35);
  Assert.That(
    transmission.CurrentGear,
    Is.EqualTo(DRIVE)
  );
  // should silently ignore
  transmission.Shift(PARK);
  Assert.That(
    transmission.CurrentGear,
    Is.EqualTo(DRIVE)
  );
  car.AccelerateTo(0); // i.e., stop
  car.BrakeToStop();

  // should work now
  transmission.Shift(PARK);
  Assert.That(
    transmission.CurrentGear,
    Is.EqualTo(PARK)
  );
}
```

The *preconditions* for a given method specify what state the world must be in for this method to run. In this case, the precondition for putting the transmission in Park is that the car's engine (a separate component elsewhere in the application's world) must be at a stop. That's a documented requirement for the method, so we want to make sure the method will behave gracefully (in this particular case, just ignore the request silently) in case the precondition is not met.

At the end of the method, *postconditions* are those things that we guarantee our method will make happen. Direct results returned by the method are one obvious thing to check, but if the method has any side effects, then we need to check those as well. In this case, applying the brakes has the side effect of stopping the car.

Some languages even have built-in support for preconditions and postconditions; interested readers might want to read about the original Eiffel in *Object-Oriented Software Construction* [Mey97] or take a look at nContract,[5] which can add similar capabilities to C#.[6]

5.5 Existence

A large number of potential bugs can be discovered by asking this key question: "Does some given thing exist?"   *CORR* **E** *CT*

For any value that's passed in or you maintain, ask yourself what would happen to the method if the value didn't exist—if it were null, blank, zero, an empty string, or an empty collection.

Many C# library methods will throw an exception of some sort when faced with nonexistent data. The problem is that it's hard to debug a generic runtime exception thrown from the depths of some library. But a specific exception that reports "Age isn't set" makes tracking down the problem much easier.

---

[5]http://puzzleware.net/nContract/nContract.html
[6]There are other efforts for other languages as well, such as http://dbc.rubyforge.org for C and http://icontract2.org for Java.

Most methods will blow up if expected data is not available, and that's probably *not* what you want them to do. So, you test for the condition—see what happens if you get a `null` instead of a `CustomerRecord` because some search failed. See what happens if the file doesn't exist or if the network is unavailable.

Ah, yes, things in the environment can wink out of existence as well—networks, files' URLs, license keys, users, printers, permissions that had been fine last time you checked—you name it. All of these things may not exist when you expect them to, so be sure to test with plenty of nulls, zeros, empty strings, and other nihilist trappings.

Make sure your method can stand up to everything, which, funnily enough, includes nothing.

5.6 Cardinality

CORRE**C**T

Cardinality has nothing to do with either highly placed religious figures or small red birds but instead with counting.

Computer programmers (your humble authors included) are really bad at counting, especially past ten when the fingers can no longer assist us. For instance, answer the following question quickly, off the top of your head, without benefit of fingers, paper, or UML:

> If you've got 12 feet of lawn that you want to fence
> and each section of fencing is 3 feet wide, how many
> fence posts do you need?

If you're like most of us, you probably answered "four" without thinking too hard about it. Pity is, that's wrong—you need five fence posts, as shown in Figure 5.1 on page 86. This model, and the subsequent common errors, come up so often that they are graced with the name *fence post errors*.

It's one of many ways you can end up being "off by one," an occasionally fatal condition that afflicts all programmers from time to time. So, you need to think about ways to test how well your method counts and check to see just how many of a thing you may have.

It's a problem related to existence, but now you want to make sure you have exactly as many as you need or that you've made exactly as many as needed. In most cases, the count of some set of values is interesting only in these three cases:

- Zero

- One

- More than one

It's called the "0–1–n rule," and it's based on the premise that if you can handle more than one of something, you can probably handle 10, 20, or 1,000 just as easily. Most of the time that's true, so many of our tests for cardinality are concerned with whether we have two or more of something. Of course, sometimes an exact count makes a difference—10 might be important to you, or 260. (Why 260? That's the defined value for MAX_PATH in windows.h, so it turns out to be a good boundary condition for finding string truncation and buffer overflow issues in underlying native code.)

Suppose we are maintaining a list of the top-ten food items ordered in a pancake house. Every time an order is taken, we have to adjust the top-ten list. We also provide the current top-ten list as a real-time data feed to the pancake boss's PDA. What sort of things might we want to test for?

- Can we produce a report when there aren't yet ten items in the list?

- Can we produce a report when there are no items on the list?

- Can we produce a report when there is only one item on the list?

- Can we add an item when there aren't yet ten items in the list (but more than one)?

- Can we add an item when there is only one item on the list?

- Can we add an item when there are already ten items on the list?

- What if there aren't ten items on the menu?

- What if there are no items on the menu?

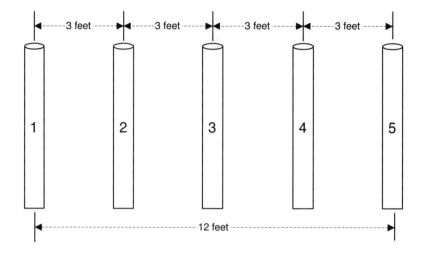

Figure 5.1: A set of fence posts

Having gone through all that, the boss now changes his mind and wants a top-twenty list instead. What do we have to change?

The correct answer is "one line," something like the following:

```
public MaxEntries {
  get { return 20; }
}
```

Now, when the boss gets overwhelmed and pleads with us to change this to be a top-five report (his PDA is pretty small, after all), we can go back and change this one number. The test should automatically follow suit, because it uses the same property.

So in the end, the tests concentrate on boundary conditions of 0, 1, and n, where n can—and will—change as the business demands.

5.7 Time

CORREC**T**

The last boundary condition in the CORRECT acronym is time. You need to keep in mind several aspects about time:

- Relative time (ordering in time)
- Absolute time (elapsed and wall clock)
- Concurrency issues

Some interfaces are inherently stateful; you expect that `Login()` will be called before `Logout()`, that `PrepareStatement()` is called before `ExecuteStatement()`, that `Connect()` is called before `Read()`, that `Read()` is called before `Close()`, and so on.

What happens if those methods are called out of order? Maybe you should try calling methods out of the expected order. Try skipping the first, last, and middle of a sequence to find these kind of temporal dependencies. Just as order of data may have mattered to you in the earlier examples (as we described in "Ordering" on page 76), now it's the order of the calling sequence of methods.

Relative time might also include issues of timeouts in the code, such as how long your method is willing to wait for some ephemeral resource to become available. As we'll discuss shortly, we'll want to exercise possible error conditions in your code, including things such as timeouts. Maybe we've got conditions that aren't guarded by timeouts—can you think of a situation where the code might get "stuck" waiting forever for something that might not happen?

This leads us to issues of elapsed time. What if something you are waiting for takes "too much" time? What if your method takes too much time to return to the caller?

Then there's the actual wall-clock time to consider. Most of the time, this makes no difference whatsoever to code. But every now and then, time of day will matter, perhaps in subtle ways. Here's a quick statement...is it true or false? "Every day of the year is 24 hours long."[7]

The answer is, "It depends." In Universal Coordinated Time (UTC), which is the modern version of Greenwich mean time (GMT), the answer is yes. In areas of the world that do not observe daylight saving time (DST), the answer is yes.

---

[7]Ignoring leap seconds for now, we're just talking about whole hours.

In most of the United States (which does observe DST), the answer is no. In March, we'll have a day with 23 hours (spring forward), and in November we'll have a day with 25 (fall back). This means arithmetic won't always work as you expect; 1:45 a.m. plus 30 minutes might equal 1:15, for instance.

But we've tested any time-sensitive code on those boundary days, right? For locations that honor DST and for those that do not?

Oh, and don't assume that any underlying library handles these issues correctly on your behalf. Unfortunately, when it comes to time, there's a lot of broken code out there. And leap seconds *do* make a difference.

Finally, one of the most insidious problems brought about by time occurs in the context of concurrency and synchronized access issues. It would take an entire book to cover designing, implementing, and debugging multithreaded, concurrent programs, so we won't take the time now to go into details, except to point out that most code you write in most languages today *will* be run in a multithreaded, multiprocessor environment (see the section on page 200 for an interesting "gotcha" in C#).

So ask yourself, what will happen if multiple threads use this same object at the same time? Are there global or instance-level data or methods that need to be synchronized? How about external access to files or hardware? Be sure to add the `lock` keyword to any property or method that needs it, and try firing off multiple threads as part of your test.

5.8 Try It Yourself

Now that we've covered the Right BICEP and CORRECT ways to come up with tests, it's your turn to try.

For each of the following examples and scenarios, write down as many possible unit tests as you can think of.

Exercises

1. **A simple stack class.** Push `String` objects onto the stack, and Pop them off according to normal stack semantics. This class provides the following methods:

Answer on 212

```
using System;
public interface StackExercise {
    /// <summary>
    /// Return and remove the most recent item from
    /// the top of the  stack.
    /// </summary>
    /// <exception cref="StackEmptyException">
    /// Throws exception if the stack is empty.
    /// </exception>
    String Pop();

    /// <summary>
    /// Add an item to the top of the stack.
    /// </summary>
    /// <param name="item">A String to push
    /// on the stack</param>
    void Push(String item);

    /// <summary>
    /// Return but do not remove the most recent
    /// item from the top of the stack.
    /// </summary>
    /// <exception cref="StackEmptyException">
    /// Throws exception if the stack is empty.
    /// </exception>
    String Top();

    /// <summary>
    /// Returns true if the stack is empty.
    /// </summary>
    bool IsEmpty();
}
```

StackExercise.cs

Here are some hints to get you started: What is likely to break? How should the stack behave when it is first initialized? How should it behave after it has been used for a while? Does it really do what it claims to do?

2. **A shopping cart.** This class lets you add, delete, and count the items in a shopping cart.

Answer on 213

What sort of boundary conditions might come up? Are there any implicit restrictions on what you can delete? Are there any interesting issues if the cart is empty?

```
public interface ShoppingCart {
    /// <summary>
    /// Add this many of this item to the
    /// shopping cart.
    /// </summary>
    /// <exception cref="ArgumentOutOfRangeException">
    /// </exception>
    void AddItems(Item anItem, int quantity);

    /// <summary>
    /// Delete this many of this item from the
    /// shopping cart
    /// </summary>
    /// <exception cref="ArgumentOutOfRangeException">
    /// </exception>
    /// <exception cref="NoSuchItemException">
    /// </exception>
    void DeleteItems(Item anItem, int quantity);

    /// <summary>
    /// Count of all items in the cart
    /// (that is, all items x qty each)
    /// </summary>
    int ItemCount { get; }

    /// Return iterator of all items
    IEnumerable GetEnumerator();
}
```

ShoppingCart.cs

Answer
on 214

3. **A fax scheduler.** This code will send faxes from a specified filename to a U.S. phone number. There is a validation requirement; a U.S. phone number with area code must be of the form *xnn-nnn-nnnn*, where x must be a digit in the range $[2..9]$ and n can be $[0..9]$. The following blocks are reserved and are not currently valid area codes: $x11$, $x9n$, $37n$, $96n$.

The method's signature is as follows:

```
///
/// Send the named file as a fax to the
/// given phone number.
/// <exception cref="MissingOrBadFileException">
/// </exception>
/// <exception cref="PhoneFormatException">
/// </exception>
/// <exception cref="PhoneAreaCodeException">
/// </exception>
public bool SendFax(String phone, String filename)
```

Given these requirements, what tests for boundary conditions can you think of?

Answer
on 215

4. **An automatic sewing machine that does embroidery.** The class that controls it takes a few basic commands. The coordinates (0,0) represent the lower-left corner of the machine.

x and y increase as you move toward the upper-right corner, whose coordinates are x = TableSize.Width - 1 and y = TableSize.Height - 1.

Coordinates are specified in fractions of centimeters.

```
public void MoveTo(double x, double y);
public void SewTo(double x, double y);
public void SetWorkpieceSize(double width,
                            double height);
public Size WorkpieceSize { get; }
public Size TableSize { get; }
```

Some real-world constraints might be interesting: you can't sew thin air, of course, and you can't sew a workpiece bigger than the machine.

Given these requirements, what boundary conditions can you think of?

5. **Audio/video-editing transport.** A class that provides methods to control a DVD or media player. There's the notion of a "current position" that lies somewhere between the beginning (historically, BOT for "beginning of tape") and the end (EOT).

Answer on 216

You can ask for the current position and move from there to another given position. *Fast-forward* moves from current position toward the EOT by some amount. *Rewind* moves from current position toward the BOT by some amount. When media is first loaded, it is positioned at BOT automatically.

```
using System;
public interface AVTransport {
   /// Move the current position ahead by this many
   /// seconds. Fast-forwarding past EOT
   /// leaves the position at EOT
   void FastForward(double seconds);

   /// Move the current position backwards by this
   /// many seconds. Rewinding past zero leaves
   /// the position at zero
   void Rewind(double seconds);

   /// Return current time position in seconds
   double CurrentTimePosition();

   /// Mark the current time position with label
   void MarkTimePosition(String name);

   /// Change the current position to the one
   /// associated with the marked name
   void GotoMark(String name);
}
```

AVTransport.cs

Answer
on 217

6. **Audio/video-editing transport, Release 2.0.** This is the same as earlier, but now you can position in seconds, minutes, or frames (there are exactly 30 frames per second in this example), and you can move relative to the beginning or the end.

Chapter 6

Using Mock Objects

The objective of unit testing is to exercise just one behavior at a time, but what happens when the method containing that behavior depends on other things—hard-to-control things such as the network, a database, or even specialized hardware?

What if our code depends on other parts of the system—maybe even *many* other parts of the system? If we're not careful, we might find ourselves writing tests that end up (directly or indirectly) initializing nearly every system component just to give the tests enough context to run. Not only is this time-consuming, but it also introduces a ridiculous amount of coupling into the testing process: someone changes an interface or a database table, and suddenly the setup code for our poor little unit test dies mysteriously. With this kind of coupling, sometimes simply adding a new test can cause other tests to fail. Even the best-intentioned developers will become discouraged after this happens a few times, and they eventually may abandon all testing. But there are techniques we can use to help.

In movie and television production, crews will often use *stand-ins* or *doubles* for the real actors. In particular, while the crews are setting up the lights and camera angles, they'll use *lighting doubles*—inexpensive, unimportant people who are about the same height and complexion as the expensive, important actors lounging safely in their luxurious trailers.

The crew then tests their setup with the lighting doubles, measuring the distance from the camera to the stand-in's nose and adjusting the lighting until there are no unwanted shadows, and so on. The obedient stand-in just stands there and doesn't whine or complain about "lacking motivation" for their character in this scene.

What we're going to do in unit testing is similar to using lighting doubles in movies. Instead of testing against the real code itself, we'll use a cheap stand-in that is kind of close to the real code, at least superficially, but will be easier to work with for our nefarious unit testing purposes.

Fortunately, there's a testing pattern that can help: *mock objects*. A mock object is simply a testing replacement for a real-world object. A number of situations can come up where mock objects can help us. Tim Mackinnon [MFC01] offers the following list:

- The real object has nondeterministic behavior (it produces unpredictable results, like a stock market quote feed or random number generator).

- The real object is difficult to set up, requiring a certain file system, database, or network environment.

- The real object has behavior that is hard to trigger (for example, a network error).

- The real object is slow.

- The real object has (or is) a user interface.

- The test needs to ask the real object about how it was used (for example, a test might need to confirm that a callback function was actually called).

- The real object does not yet exist (a common problem when interfacing with other teams or new hardware systems).

Using mock objects, we can get around all of these problems. The three key steps to using mock objects for testing are as follows:

1. Use an interface to describe the relevant methods on the object.

2. Implement the interface for production code.

3. Implement the interface in a mock object for testing.

The code under test refers to an object only by its interface or base class, so it can remain blissfully ignorant about whether it is using the real object or the mock. Sometimes there's a simpler solution to getting on with our testing, so let's explore that first.

6.1 Stubs

What we need to do is stub out all those uncooperative parts of the real world and replace them with more complicit allies— our own version of lighting doubles. For example, stubs allow us to fake our interaction with a database or the file system.

In many cases, stubs just implement an interface and return dummy values for the methods in said interface. Note that although we can also extract an abstract class, interfaces are preferred since they have no implementation details and therefore provide the loosest coupling.[1] In even simpler cases, all the implemented methods in the stub just throw a NotImplementedException.[2]

A common scenario is when there is a class that encapsulates database access[3] but we don't want to configure and populate a real-world database to run simple tests that operate only on data.

```
public class MySqlCustomerRepository
{
  public string[] FindById(long id)
  {
    //xxx xx xxxxx
  }
}
```

---

[1]See [Pug06] and [CA05] for more details on designing with interfaces.

[2]Most IDEs will fill in this exception for us when told to automatically implement the methods for an interface.

[3]The Repository design pattern documented in [Fow03] is one way to accomplish this.

First, we extract an interface for the methods we need to stub
and apply that interface to the class we want to mock:

```
public interface CustomerRepository
{
  string[] FindById(long id);
}
public class MySqlCustomerRepository : CustomerRepository
{
  public string[] FindById(long id)
  {
    ...
  }
}
```

Next, we can return the dummy value that we think will evoke
the behavior we want from the ProductAdoptionService:

```
public class StubCustomerRepository : CustomerRepository
{
  public string[] FindById(long id)
  {
    return null;
  }
}
```

For now we put the code for this stub class in the same file
as the test fixture class that will be using it. Later we'll move
it to a more general area where other test fixture classes can
access it. Let's plug in the stub to our unit test like so:

```
namespace WebCRM.Test.ProductAdoptionTest
{
  [TestFixture]
  public class NoDataFixture
  {
    [Test]
    public void OverallRateIsZero()
    {
      CustomerRepository customerRepository =
        new StubCustomerRepository();
      ProductAdoptionService service =
        new ProductAdoptionService(customerRepository);
      Assert.That(service.GetPercentage(), Is.EqualTo(0));
    }
  }
}
```

Oops, this won't actually compile. We get an error similar to
this:

```
Argument 1: Cannot convert from
  'CustomerRepository' to 'MySqlCustomerRepository'
```

The `ProductAdoptionService` is still expecting an instance of the concrete `MySqlCustomerRepository` class as the parameter to its constructor. We'll need to change that parameter to accept an object that implements the `CustomerRepository` interface instead. We'll also need to change the field in the `ProductAdoptionService`:

```
public class ProductAdoptionService
{
  CustomerRepository repository;
  public ProductAdoptionService(CustomerRepository repository)
  {
    this.repository = repository;
  }
  xxxxx xx xxxxx xx
}
```

If we're lucky, our test might now pass, and we didn't have to touch a database. In fact, this test could have been written before there was a schema design, database vendor debate, or anything else. By programming to interfaces, we can plug in what we need without being blocked on politicking or other noncoding activities that can slow down a project. Note that we not only get to verify the code being tested produces the results that we want, but we also get to verify that it *interacts* with the stubbed class in the way we expect.

6.2 Fakes

Sometimes you need to do more than return a single, static dummy value to get at the code you're trying to test. Fakes, sometimes known as *static* or *hand-rolled mocks*, improve on stubs by allowing for several different values to be returned. What if you have files on the file system that conform to a certain format and you want to test that you're parsing them correctly?

```
public class DumpFileParser
{
  FileStream stream;
  public DumpFileParser(string fileName)
  {
    stream = File.Open(fileName);
  }
  xxxx xxx xxxx
}
```

The previous code requires a real file on the file system in order to be tested. This can put an unnecessary file system layout burden on the person running the tests, and the disk I/O will slow down the tests.[4] What can you do in a situation like this to make it easier to test? In this case, the class actually discards the supplied filename after the constructor and just operates on the resulting stream.

We'll look at a suboptimal way of making it more testable and then at a more optimal way. It's good to understand what the evils in the world are so that we don't accidentally end up evoking any of them.

What if we used #define to tell the code when we were testing? Then it wouldn't use the file system.

```
public class DumpFileParser
{
  FileStream stream;
  public DumpFileParser(string fileName)
  {
#if TESTING
  stream = new MemoryStream();
#else
  stream = File.Open(fileName);
#endif
  }
  xxx. xx. xxx.
}
```

MemoryStream is a nifty class in the .NET class library that allows us to make, as you may have guessed, an in-memory stream. Now we have a real Stream-derived object that the class can interact with, and it doesn't touch the file system. Before we get too far ahead of ourselves, though, realize that an empty stream has limitations. First, an empty stream doesn't really help you if the code needs to read data from that stream. Many of the tests you write will probably want to supply different data via the stream to make sure the parser behaves correctly. We could figure out various ways to get some test data into place in this scenario, but this approach works around that the code wants the stream to be parameterized; our attempt to test this code has illuminated this.

---

[4]This doesn't seem like a big deal, but little slowdowns like this add up quickly.

Also, #if statements strewn throughout the code for testing purposes are difficult to maintain. And, in our opinion, they're ugly to boot.

It might also be tempting to just add an empty constructor to eliminate the need for any of this deep thinking. Although this would "work" in a very narrow sense, there's a good reason there wasn't an empty constructor in the first place: without the Stream being created, the object isn't in a valid state. In this case, invalid state means a probable NullReferenceException whenever you try to do anything with the object. Objects being in a valid state after construction is a core object-oriented design principle, and ignoring it is not the right thing to do in this case. Tests can help drive improvements to the code's design, but this particular example isn't one of them.

Now that we've discussed what won't work, what will work? What if we shifted the responsibility of actually getting the FileStream to the consumers of this class and those consumers passed in a FileStream to the constructor instead of a filename? Doing this transformation would resolve the design feedback we're getting from testing this in the first place:

```
public class DumpFileParser
{
  Stream stream;
  public DumpFileParser(Stream dumpStream)
  {
    this.stream = dumpStream;
  }
  x.x.x.  x.x.x.  x.x.x.
}
```

This isn't bad at all. Now the consumers of the class, including the tests, could perform the File.Open() and pass in a FileStream. It may seem like we're just moving the problem around, but we needed to make our code a little shy; specifically, we needed to make it more liberal in what it will accept without complaint.[5] In this case, we aren't using any methods specific to FileStream, so the constructor can actually accept the base class, Stream, instead.[6]

---

[5]See [HT00] for details on why and how to make code "shy."

[6]You generally want to use interfaces instead of abstract classes for parameters, but Stream doesn't have a base interface [CA05].

What does that get us? Well, in our tests we can now use the spiffy MemoryStream class, like so:

```
[TestFixture]
public class DumpFileParserTest
{
  private StreamWriter writer;
  private DumpFileParser parser;
  private MemoryStream stream;
  [SetUp]
  public void SetUp()
  {
    stream = new MemoryStream();
    writer = new StreamWriter(stream);
  }
  [Test]
  public void EmptyLine()
  {
    writer.WriteLine(string.Empty);
    parser = new Parser(stream);
    Assert.That(xxxx, xxx),
  }
}
```

Presto! We now have an instant pseudo text file that we can also use to write binary data. Since this operates in memory, we won't incur the performance penalty of disk I/O. Note that this technique works just as well with sockets and other stream-based I/O. Now we can do the testing we need, quickly and conveniently. A nice side effect is that our code is more loosely coupled, yielding a more flexible design that is easier to reuse. One could say that changing the parameter to a Stream was a change strictly for the sake of testing, and that observation would be somewhat correct. The other side of the story is that by not programming against a concrete implementation, the code now has a more flexible design. We were led to this by refactoring a very little bit to make things easier to test. This kind of design feedback is the real magic of unit testing, but this is only one simple example.

Faking Collaborators

The DumpFileParser class we were just working on does some pretty complicated collation of the data in the stream. If another class depends on DumpFileParser, we don't want to make the entire fake stream necessary for it to produce the data against which we're trying to test our other class. Besides that it would be really tedious, it adds a whole new dimension of coupling and maintenance to the test code. If we use a real `DumpFileParser` while testing a collaborating class, we're increasing the work we have to do if `DumpFileParser` changes or gets removed.

That doesn't sound very pragmatic, so how do we decouple `DumpFileParser` from the tests of a class that requires a `DumpFileParser`? It's actually similar to our initial example—we need to abstract things up a level, and then we can supply a variation on `DumpFileParser` that returns whatever dummy values we need for the purpose of testing the other object. This is known in some circles as creating a *fake* and in other circles as a *static mock*. Let's look at some code:

```csharp
public class Analyzer
{
  private DumpFileParser parser;
  private List<string> reportItems;
  public Analyzer(DumpFileParser parser)
  {
    this.parser = parser;
  }
  public bool ExpectationsMet
  {
    get
    {
      return
        parser.ReportItems.Count == reportItems.Count;
    }
  }
  public byte[] GetNextInstruction()
  {
    //.../.x.x/.../.x
  }
}
```

If we wanted to test the `ExpectationsMet` property, the `ReportItems` property on `parser` would need to be under our control so we can make it return what we want. One way would be to make the `ReportItems` property on `DumpFileParser` virtual. We could then subclass and override it for our testing purposes and pass an instance of said subclass into the constructor for `Analyzer`.

Although that would work, there's a better way that yields a more flexible, and interface-oriented, design: extract an interface called `Parsable` that contains, for the time being, a declaration for the `ReportItems` property getter:

```
public interface Parsable
{
  List<string> ReportItems
  {
    get;
  }
}
```

Then, we can make `DumpFileParser` implement the `Parsable` interface. Next, we change the `Analyzer` constructor's parameter from `DumpFileParser` to `Parsable`. Last, we change the `parser` field in `Analyzer` from the `DumpFileParser` concrete class to be the `Parsable` interface that `DumpFileParser` now implements. When we try to compile, the compiler might tell us that we're using some methods not defined on the `Parsable` interface. We'll need to add those methods to the interface as well:

```
public DumpFileParser : Parsable
{
  x x / : x x x
}
public class Analyzer
{
  private Parsable parser;
  private List<string> reportItems;
  public Analyzer(Parsable parser)
  {
    this.parser = parser;
  }
  x x / : x x x /
}
```

None of the existing consumers of `Analyzer` has to change, and yet, we have just made `Analyzer` easier to test *and* reuse. If we wanted to add the ability to parse another file format, `Analyzer` itself wouldn't have to change to accommodate the extra functionality—only the consumers would by passing in a new class that implemented the `Parsable` interface.

This is a good example of the advantage of interface-based design, but the point worth mentioning again is that we arrived at this better design by refactoring toward testability. Besides being more testable and reusable, it also means we don't need to wait for another set of programmers to finish implementing the concrete class that our class might be collaborating with. We can fully unit test our class by faking the collaborator's interface, which generally makes integrating with the concrete classes developed by others (or even our future selves) significantly less painful.[7]

Fakes are great, especially when they're simple, but it's also easy to outgrow them, such as when we need to do more than return a single value, for instance. At some point, we want to return values in a certain order each time a method is called. To accomplish this with a fake, we would need to track a `Stack` of return values for a given method:

```
public class FakeParser : Parsable
{
  private Stack<byte[]> bytesToReturn;
  public Stack<byte[]> BytesToReturn
  {
    get { return bytesToReturn; }
    set { bytesToReturn = value; }
  }
  public Boolean ExpectationsMet
  {
    get { return false; }
  }
  public Byte[] GetNextInstruction()
  {
    return BytesToReturn.Pop();
  }
}
```

Although this would work and is a clever way to make a programmable fake, we risk repeating ourselves because we would end up doing this for most methods on our fake. It also gets a little hairier when we have to make them throw specific exceptions at certain points to test failure modes. Surely, there must be a better way.

---

[7]In many cases, the usually pandemonious step of integration just works.

6.3 Mock Objects

Sometimes we'll need to test something that uses an existing interface when there are no prewritten stubs or fakes lying around. Often, we can just jump right on in and create a new fake.

But what if the interface that we're mocking is enormous, with dozens of methods and accessors? That could mean a lot of work producing a fake that implements the interface. This is particularly galling if we need only one or two methods from the interface to run our tests, and we can't refactor to break up the interface for some reason.

This is where dynamic mock objects come in. They let us create an object that responds as if it implemented a full interface, but in reality it is totally generic. You need to tell this object only how to respond to the method calls that our code uses. This can represent a considerable savings in time. It'll also give you less code to maintain in the future.

Dynamic mocks are great, but they also make it easy to work around design issues rather than refactoring to fix them. With fakes, because they are hand-rolled, kinks in the design of the code we're trying to test are more obvious.

Some people prefer using hand-rolled fakes and stubs whenever possible so they can get design feedback more directly. Do whatever you are most comfortable with, but pay close attention to what the code is trying to tell you.

The dynamic mock packages operate by creating *proxy objects* that implement the mocked interface at runtime in the underlying implementation. These are objects that are designed to stand in for their real-world counterparts. In the dynamic mock object context, this means we can use a proxy in place of a real object in our tests.

However, we still need to be able to control this generated proxy object—we need to be able to tell it how to respond. This is where the controller comes in.

The controller is in charge of a dynamic mock object. We use the controller to create an instance of the mock and to tell the mock what to do. This is referred to as *programming* the mock. Sometimes the controller is told directly as in NUnit's mocks, and sometimes it is told indirectly as in the NMock2 framework, which we'll discuss later in the chapter.

In the old days, just having the ability to call subroutines was a great advance. Then libraries of code became popular— everything had to be library. Nowadays, libraries aren't good enough. You need a *framework* to be taken seriously.

In the case of .NET, you can choose from several alternative mock object frameworks. (You can find a good list on the website at `http://www.mockobjects.com.`)

NUnit includes its own built-in framework that the NUnit team uses to test NUnit itself. NUnit's mock framework doesn't provide all the features of some other frameworks, so we'll look at a few other frameworks as well.

But before we do, it's worth noting that because we're in the common language runtime (CLR) environment, this same framework can be used to mock objects for any code written in any language compliant with the ECMA Common Language Specification (CLS).

NUnit Mocks

When you think about it, there's really not too much to a mock object: it's simply an object that implements a particular interface, returns values we want it to return, and checks that it was used in a certain way. As a result, the basic frameworks for creating mock objects are also simple.

In the previous section, we saw what we would have to go through to have our fake be somewhat programmable and return multiple values for a given method call. Here is how we would do this using NUnit's mock framework.

Note that to compile this code, we'll have to add a reference to the `nunit.mocks.dll` assembly *in addition to* the `nunit.framework.dll` reference:

```
using NUnit.Framework;
using NUnit.Framework.SyntaxHelpers;
using NUnit.Mocks;

[TestFixture]
public class AnalyzerTest
{
  Analyzer analyzer;
  Parsable parser;

  [Test]
  public void NoBytes()
  {
    DynamicMock controller =
      new DynamicMock(typeof(Parsable));
    parser = controller.MockInstance as Parsable;
    analyzer = new Analyzer(parser);

    controller.ExpectAndReturn(
      "GetNextInstruction",// method name
      new byte[] {},       // return value
      null                 // expected arguments
    );

    controller.ExpectAndReturn(
      "get_ExpectedReportItems",
      new List<string>(),
      null
    );

    analyzer.Run();

    Assert.That(analyzer.ReportItems, Is.Empty);

    controller.Verify();//fails if expectations are unmet
  }
}
```

Mock object frameworks make it easy to set multiple method call expectations, with or without accompanying dummy values that should be returned, with or without throwing exceptions, and so on. In the previous code, we first instantiate a DynamicMock object, passing the Parsable interface's type into the constructor. We can create a DynamicMock only for interfaces or classes that derive from MarshalByRefObject because of various reasons that we won't go into here. If you're curious, check out the section on remoting in [Ric06] and the source code for NUnit mocks in NUnit's source code distribution.

We highly recommend using interfaces whenever possible, even if you have to extract them. This recommendation is not only for the reasons of good design previously discussed in this chapter but also because of the complex implications of deriving from `MarshalByRefObject`. Again, see [Ric06] for details on `MarshalByRefObject`.

Once the mock is created, we pass it in to the real object with which we are testing the interaction. Since we're focusing on testing the interaction after `Run()` is called, we start programming it with our expectations right before the call to `Run`, since this expresses our intentions clearly. To put it another way, we *don't* want to program all the expectations for our mock in a big clump that is difficult to read and understand. In the previous code, the expectations we set are as follows:

- The method name

- The value, if any, that will be returned when the mocked method is called

- The specific arguments, if any, we expect the mocked method to be called with

After creating the mock, we tell it to expect a call to `Get-NextInstruction()` and to return an empty `byte` array. The final `null` parameter indicates there are no specific method argument expectations. In this case, the method in question doesn't have any parameters, but we can also supply `null` when we just don't care. In our experience, checking specific arguments supplied to the mocked method is usually unnecessary because that level of detail usually is unnecessary to express the intention of the interaction we're testing.

Next, we tell the mock to expect a call to the getter for the `Ex-pectedReportItems` property. Note that we had to prepend `get_` to the property name.[8] If we were expecting a call to the setter, we would prepend `set_`.

We then get our mock object via the `MockInstance` property. Because NUnit's mock framework doesn't take advantage of

---

[8]For more details on the inner workings of properties, see [Ric06].

generics, we have to cast it—which is why we use the as operator. At that point, we can treat that instance like the real object as long as we use it only in the way we programmed it. One way to think about it is the framework provides a kind of API-level record-and-playback mechanism. If we didn't "record" the method calls, the mock can't "play" them back.

By default, the DynamicMock operates fairly loosely. Just by telling the mock to expect the method call once, the mock will happily do whatever we told it to, even if the method is called multiple times. It also doesn't care about the order in which the expected methods are called by default. We sometimes don't care about that level of detail, and that makes this default behavior quite nice.

That being said, it is common to want to fail a test if calls on the mock don't happen in a certain order. For instance, we might want to make sure that a call to Close happens last. In cases like that, setting the Strict property is highly encouraged.

When we want that vigilance, we can set the Strict property on the mock to true. One thing the strict flag does is make the mock fail the test immediately if something happens that wasn't expected. If we're not using strict mode, then we need to ask the mock to verify that all the expectations were met. The Verify method acts as a kind of assertion. If something we told the mock to expect didn't happen, the verification will fail. Since the verification generally happens at the end of the test, it can sometimes be difficult to track down where things went wrong.

To keep things sane, keep your interaction tests short and sweet. If you find yourself programming a lot of mocks or a single mock with a lot of method calls, stop coding and listen to the design feedback the test is giving you—a refactoring may be in order. Some common scenarios where this issue comes up is when the interfaces' methods or objects' responsibilities are too granular. Combining the methods or objects to be slightly higher level may help resolve the issue of overly verbose mock setup.

Note that the `ExpectAndReturn` methods take the method name as a `string` parameter. This introduces a gotcha where renaming the method in the code, but not in the mock expectation, will cause an exception to be thrown when the test containing the mock is run. Other frameworks, which we'll discuss later in this chapter, improve upon this limitation.

Some of the other expectations we can set using NUnit's `DynamicMock` include the following:

- `ExpectNoCall(string methodName)`, which will cause verification to fail if the method supplied is called. If the mock is in strict mode, the test will fail immediately if the specified method is called.

- `ExpectAndThrow(string methodName, Exception exception, params object[] args)`, which operates the same as `ExpectAndReturn`, except the specified exception is thrown. This is great for making sure your exception handling interaction between classes is rock solid and stays that way.

- `SetReturnValue(string methodName, object returnValue)`, which will always return the value specified no matter how many times the method in question is called. We generally don't recommend using this, because it can cover up the very interaction feedback that mocks are so good at giving us.

For more information, check out NUnit's documentation, or just explore a bit with a method-completing code editor.

NMock2 Framework

NMock2,[9] which is based on jMock for Java,[10] inspired NUnit's new style of constraint-based assertions. It is meant to provide a more concise and easily readable syntax in contrast to other mock frameworks. Since we use unit tests as documentation for our code, it's important that the configuration of our mocks be easy to read and understand.

---

[9]http://nmock.org
[10]http://jmock.org

In that vein, NMock's syntax reads from left to right, albeit with a syntax that might look a bit strange at first:

```
using NUnit.Framework;
using NMock2;

[TestFixture]
public class AnalyzerTest
{
  Analyzer analyzer;
  Parsable parser;
  Mockery mockery;

  [Test]
  public void NoBytes()
  {
    mockery = new Mockery();
    parser = mockery.NewMock<Parsable>();
    analyzer = new Analyzer(parser);

    Expect.Once.On(parser)
      .Method("GetNextInstruction")
      .Will(Return.Value(new byte[] {}));

    Expect.Once.On(parser)
      .GetProperty("ExpectedReportItems")
      .Will(Return.Value(new List<string>()));

    analyzer.Run();

    Assert.That(
      analyzer.ReportItems,
      new EmptyConstraint()
    );

    mockery.VerifyAllExpectationsHaveBeenMet();
  }
}
```

This code is equivalent to the code from the previous subsection that was written using NUnit's mocks. First, we create a Mockery object. Mockery acts as a factory for mock objects,[11] via the NewMock<T>() generic method. Because it is a generic method, whatever type we parameterize it with is the type it will return. This allows us to avoid the casting we had to do in NUnit's mocks.[12] Note that the use of a generic method is a C# 2.0 feature, so NMock2 can't be used on a project that strictly uses an earlier C# version. The Mockery object also keeps track of the expectations we are setting.

---

[11]Mocks + Factory = Mockery, get it?

[12]The NUnit 2.4 team purposefully restrained themselves to using only C# 1.1 features so it could be more widely used.

We then set up the expectations. Remember, we program the mock only with the minimal number of expectations we need to test the interaction aspect of the behavior. We want this to read like a conversation between the mock and the real object, from A to B and back again. We expect that, only once, the parser's `GetNextInstruction` method will be called, and it will return an empty `byte` array. Under the covers, the expectations are communicated to the `Mockery` object, which created the `Parser` mock in the first place.

To our subjective eyes, NMock2 reads a bit more easily than other frameworks. It allows us to focus on only the aspects that we care about. On the other hand, NUnit's mocks require us always to provide the arguments we are expecting. For instance, we have to supply `null` to tell it we don't have any argument expectations. In NMock2, we add the argument constraint only if we actually need it by adding `.With(x)` to the chain. This extra flexibility seems small, but it adds up to test code that is easier to maintain.

One major caveat is that we can no longer use NUnit's `AssertionHelpers` namespace, which gave us `Is` and `Has`, amongst other nice things, because NMock2 also defines classes with those names. We're not using them in this example, because they relate to argument matching.

Because of this conflict, we're using `new EmptyConstraint()` instead of the usual `Is.Empty`. We could also substitute in the classic-style assertion, `CollectionAssert.IsEmpty()`. Let's hope this namespace issue will be resolved in future versions so everyone can use both NUnit and NMock2 to their fullest advantage.

DotNetMock Framework

Some objects are difficult to set up mocks for, regardless of the framework, because of the complexity and girth of their interfaces. ASP.NET and ADO.NET objects can be fairly difficult in particular. In these cases, a library of static mocks that are engineered specifically for common unit testing scenarios can come in handy.

> ## Joe Asks...
>
> ### How Do I Mock Singletons?
>
> With design patterns becoming popular, many projects have various patterns implemented as part of their designs. One of the most commonly misunderstood patterns is the singleton.
>
> Unfortunately, it is usually misimplemented in such a way that introduces global state that changes over the course of the program; this in turn introduces a large amount of temporal coupling, hidden dependencies, and extremely difficult debugging. Many times, a singleton isn't even necessary, but it can be a tempting way to cheat without actually improving the design.
>
> In the next section, we'll show how to test around a usage of `DateTime.Now`, which is a static global, just like a singleton class can be. The key is to extract an interface for the methods actually used by the consumers of the singleton class and then extract a parameter from the class or method that accepts the interface for the singleton. From that point, you can create a mock from the extracted interface, passing in the mock via the parameter.
>
> Even if you aren't unit testing, this is the standard set of refactorings for loosening the hangman's knot of singletons that many projects get themselves into. Once you see the real dependencies of the extracted parameters, you'll be able to improve your design instead of working around it. When applying this design feedback, you may find that the singleton is simply no longer necessary.

> ### RhinoMock
>
> There's another option in the world of mock frameworks that some of our reviewers asked us to mention: RhinoMock.[a] RhinoMock distinguishes itself by using real method calls to specify expectations, instead of strings. It is this simple feature that makes RhinoMock work more easily with code completion and refactoring capabilities in modern IDEs.
>
> Each framework has advantages and disadvantages; which one you end up applying on your project is a matter of preference and practicality. We do encourage you to try a couple before settling, though.
>
> ---
>
> [a]http://www.ayende.com/projects/rhino-mocks.aspx

To meet this need, the DotNetMock[13] framework is actually three things in one:

- It's a framework (not surprisingly), allowing us to create mock objects in a structured way.

- It contains a (small) set of predefined mock objects that we can use out of the box to test our application.

- Finally, it comes with a technology, dynamic mocks, that lets us construct mock objects without all that messy coding.

We recommend using one of the aforementioned mock object frameworks for standard mock program activities and using DotNetMock for when you need to mock one of the messier framework classes (like those in the ADO.NET and ASP.NET technologies). As such, we're going to cover only the library of mocks that comes with DotNetMock.

---

[13]http://dotnetmock.sourceforge.net

Supplied Mock Objects

One of the nice features of using a standardized framework for testing is that we can start to build a library of standard mock objects and reuse these across projects. In fact, in the open source world, you might even find that other folks have mocked up the interfaces you need and made them freely available. The DotNetMock package comes with a (small) number of these off-the-shelf mock object packages, available in DotNetMock.Framework. Although DotNetMock's library of predefined mocks hasn't been updated for .NET 2.0 at the time of this writing, it's still useful if you're using .NET 1.1 APIs. Here we'll look at one of these, DotNetMock.Framework.Data, which implements many of the interfaces in .NET's System.Data.

Let's start by implementing more of our access controller. After verifying that a password has been supplied, we'll now go to a database table and verify that a row exists giving this user—identified with the given password—access to our resource.

```
using System;
using System.Data;
using System.Data.SqlClient;
public class AccessController1 {
  private ILogger      logger;
  private String       resource;
  private IDbConnection conn;

  public static readonly String CHECK_SQL =
    "select count(*) from access where " +
    "user=@user and password=@password " +
    "and resource=@resource";

  public AccessController1(String resource,
                           ILogger logger,
                           IDbConnection conn) {
    this.logger   = logger;
    this.resource = resource;
    this.conn     = conn;
    logger.SetName("AccessControl");
  }

  public bool CanAccess(String user, String password) {
    logger.Log("Checking access for " + user +
      " to " + resource);

    if (password == null || password.Length == 0) {
      logger.Log("Missing password. Access denied");
      return false;
    }
```

```
        IDbCommand cmd = conn.CreateCommand();
        cmd.CommandText = CHECK_SQL;
        cmd.Parameters.Add(
          new SqlParameter("@user",     user));
        cmd.Parameters.Add(
          new SqlParameter("@password", password));
        cmd.Parameters.Add(
          new SqlParameter("@resource", resource));
        IDataReader rdr = cmd.ExecuteReader();

        int rows = 0;

        if (rdr.Read())
          rows = rdr.GetInt32(0);

        cmd.Dispose();

        if (rows == 1) {
          logger.Log("Access granted");
          return true;
        }
        else {
          logger.Log("Access denied");
          return false;
        }
      }
    }
```

AccessController1.cs

The test code for this is somewhat more complicated than the previous cases, mostly because we want to knit together all the various objects used to access the database (the connection, the command, the various parameters, and the reader that returns the result).

We also want to set up a reasonable set of expectations to ensure that the underlying code is calling the database layer correctly.

```
Line 1  using DotNetMock.Framework.Data;
        using NUnit.Framework;
        using NUnit.Framework.SyntaxHelpers;
        using System;
     5
        [TestFixture]
        public class AnotherAccessControllerTest
        {
          [Test]
    10    public void ValidUser()
          {
            MockLogger3 logger = new MockLogger3();
            logger.ExpectedName = "AccessControl";
            logger.AddExpectedMsg(
    15        "Checking access for dave to secrets");
            logger.AddExpectedMsg("Access granted");
```

```
         -      // set up the mock database
         -      MockDbConnection conn = new MockDbConnection();
        20      MockCommand cmd = new MockCommand();
         -      MockDataReader rdr = new MockDataReader();

         -      conn.SetExpectedCommand(cmd);
         -      cmd.SetExpectedCommandText(
        25        AccessController1.CHECK_SQL);
         -      cmd.SetExpectedExecuteCalls(1);
         -      cmd.SetExpectedParameter(
         -        new MockDataParameter("@user",      "dave"));
         -      cmd.SetExpectedParameter(
        30        new MockDataParameter("@password", "shhh"));
         -      cmd.SetExpectedParameter(
         -        new MockDataParameter("@resource", "secrets"));

         -      cmd.SetExpectedReader(rdr);
        35      object [,] rows = new object[1,1];
         -      rows[0, 0] = 1;
         -      rdr.SetRows(rows);

         -      AccessController1 access =
        40        new AccessController1("secrets", logger, conn);

         -      Assert.That(
         -        access.CanAccess("dave", "shhh"),
         -        Is.True
        45      );
         -      logger.Verify();
         -      conn.Verify();
         -      cmd.Verify();
         -    }
        50  }
```

On line 1 we bring in the DotNetMock framework's Data components. In the body of the test method, we start by creating and setting up a mock logger as before. At line 19 we create three mock database objects: the connection, a command (used to issue SQL queries into the database), and a reader (used to return the results of a query).

We now need to bind these three objects together. Line 23 tells the connection object that when it is asked to generate a command object, it should return our mock command object, cmd. We then set up that command object's expectations: the SQL it should receive, the number of times it will be executed, and the parameters it should expect to receive.

Line 34 starts the stanza that sets up the reader object. It is first associated with the command (so that when the mock command is executed, it will return this reader object).

> ## It Isn't All Perfect
>
> Observant readers may be wondering why our new `AccessController` class went to the trouble of using a `Reader` object to get the count back from executing the query. Why didn't we just use the `ExecuteScalar` method of the command object to return the count directly?
>
> Unfortunately, the mock object implementation of `IDbCommand` isn't quite complete (at least at the time of writing). Although `ExecuteScalar` is implemented, it always returns a `null` value. This means we couldn't use it in our tests.

We then set up its result set, a two-dimensional array of objects containing the rows returned by the query and the columns in each row. In our case, the result set contains just a single row containing a single column, the count, but we still need to wrap it in the two-dimensional array.

Finally, on line 39, we create our access controller and check to see whether "dave" can access the resource "secrets" by using the password "shhh." Because these values correspond to the values we set up for the query, the access controller will be able to use our mock database objects, which will return a count of 1, and the access will be accepted. At the end of the test, we then verify that the logger, connection, and command mock objects were used correctly by our method under test.

6.4 When Not to Mock

Mock objects are an appealing technology, but because they involve writing code, they represent a definite cost to a project. Whenever you find yourself thinking that you want to write a mock object to help with testing, stop and consider alternatives for a couple of seconds. In particular, ask yourself the following question: "Will a refactoring eliminate the need for a mock object?"

As a (somewhat contrived) example, let's imagine we're writing code that downloads files to a handheld device over a relatively slow wire. Because of some hardware restrictions, after we've sent a block of data, we have to wait a while before trying to talk with the device again. The length of time we have to wait depends on the amount of data sent—the hardware guys gave us a table of values to use.

We might start off by writing a routine that waits a length of time dependent on the size of data sent:

```csharp
public void WaitForData(int dataSize)
{
  int timeToWait;
  if (dataSize < 100)
  {
    timeToWait = 50;
  }
  else if (dataSize < 250)
  {
    timeToWait = 100;
  }
  else
  {
    timeToWait = 200;
  }
  Thread.Sleep(timeToWait);
}
```

Example.cs

Now we want to test this method, but there's a problem. The only way to see whether it works is to check to see whether it sleeps for the right amount of time for various values of the dataSize parameters. That's not an easy test to write: we'd have to build in a *fudge factor*, because the time we measure for the wait won't be exact. We might even have to set up some kind of watchdog thread to ensure that the sleep doesn't go on too long. There's also the elapsed time to consider. If running our tests causes Thread.Sleep to be called multiple times, our unit tests will take longer to complete—which won't increase our popularity amongst co-workers.

After reading this chapter, your first thought might be to solve these problems using a mock object. If we wrap Thread with some kind of wrapper object and then mock that wrapper, we can verify that its Sleep method was called with the expected values. This would work, but it would add more code—a wrapper object and the test code that programs the mock.

This is the time to reflect: could we redesign our code slightly to make it easier to test? Of course we could!

```csharp
public int HowLongToWait(int dataSize)
{
  int timeToWait;
  if (dataSize < 100)
  {
    timeToWait = 50;
  }
  else if (dataSize < 250)
  {
    timeToWait = 100;
  }
  else
  {
    timeToWait = 200;
  }
  return timeToWait;
}
public void WaitForData(int dataSize)
{
  Thread.Sleep(HowLongToWait(dataSize));
}
```

Example.cs

In this code we've split the waiting into two methods. One calculates the number of milliseconds to wait based on the data's size, and the other calls it to get the parameter to pass to Thread.Sleep.

If we assume that the framework Sleep method works, then there's probably no need to test this second method. We can eyeball it and see it does what it says it should. That leaves us with the simple task of testing the behavior that calculates the time to wait:

```csharp
[Test]
void WaitTimes()
{
  Waiter w = new Waiter();
  Assert.That(w.HowLongToWait(0), Is.EqualTo(50));
  Assert.That(w.HowLongToWait(99), Is.EqualTo(50));
  Assert.That(w.HowLongToWait(100), Is.EqualTo(100));
  Assert.That(w.HowLongToWait(249), Is.EqualTo(100));
  Assert.That(w.HowLongToWait(250), Is.EqualTo(200));
  Assert.That(w.HowLongToWait(251), Is.EqualTo(200));
}
```

Example.cs

A simple refactoring has led us to a better design and eliminated a whole lot of pain associated with coding up the tests.

Testing for Time

Here's another real-world example that shows how a simple refactoring makes for both an easier test and a better, more decoupled design. This is the code to be tested; note the dependency on the current system time:

```
public static string DaysFromNow(DateTime last)
{
  TimeSpan span = DateTime.Now - last;

  switch (span.Days)
  {
    case 0:
      return "Today";
    case 1:
      return "Yesterday";
    default:
      return span.Days + " days ago";
  }
}
```

On this particular project, one senior engineer spent a lot of time trying to invent a good way to fake out or change `Date-Time.Now`. But then an intern from Portugal who learned C# via a few test-driven development books saw the code and made the obvious suggestion of extracting a parameter [FBB+99]. It took some time for the senior engineer to recover from a bad case of "bruised ego," but everyone agreed it made the code better.

The code was refactored to look like the following:

```
public static
string DaysFromNow(DateTime current, DateTime last)
{
  TimeSpan span = current - last;

  switch (span.Days)
  {
    case 0:
      return "Today";
    case 1:
      return "Yesterday";
    default:
      return span.Days + " days ago";
  }
}
```

Notice there is no dependency on the current date or time anywhere in the code; it is passed in from the caller.

Now we can use a simple test to drive this code:

```
[Test]
public void Yesterday()
{
  DateTime date = new DateTime(2007, 9, 27);
  DateTime dateMinusOneDay = new DateTime(2007, 9, 26);
  Assert.That(
    DaysFromNow(date, dateMinusOneDay),
    Is.EqualTo("Yesterday")
  );
}
```

Sometimes we can't change your existing interfaces to accept the parameterized singleton or just want to do things in a more incremental fashion so we don't have to upheave the entire code base. In that case, add a new interface that adds the parameterized singleton, and then have the original interface delegate to the new one:

```
public static string DaysFromNow(DateTime last)
{
  return DaysFromNow(DateTime.Now, last);
}
```

We *will* eventually want to get rid of this delegation when practical, of course.

And that's all there is to mock objects: fake out parts of the real world so we can concentrate on testing our own code. This generally has the nice side effect of improving our design. Some people might perceive that testing with fakes and mocks makes the testing less "real," but as you can see through the examples, the *interaction* aspects of the behavior being tested are as real as anything else. They would be difficult and slow to reproduce accurately in the real world.

Also, remember that it's called *unit testing* for a reason. We don't drag the whole system along for the ride because we want to test one behavior of a single class. This is true even if the behavior we want to test is the interaction with other classes.

## Chapter 7

Properties of Good Tests

Unit tests are very powerful magic, and if used badly, they can cause an enormous amount of damage to a project by wasting time. In fact, you can easily waste so much time maintaining and debugging the tests themselves that the production code—and the whole project—suffers.

We can't let that happen. Remember, the whole reason we're unit testing in the first place is to make our lives easier! Fortunately, we need to follow only a few simple guidelines to keep trouble from brewing on our projects.

Good tests have the following properties, which makes them A TRIP:

- **A**utomatic

- **T**horough

- **R**epeatable

- **I**ndependent

- **P**rofessional

Let's look at what each of these properties means to us.

7.1 Automatic

Unit tests need to run automatically. We mean "automatically" in two ways: invoking the tests and checking the results.

Automatic Invocation

It must be really easy for you to invoke one or more unit tests because you will be doing it all day long, day in and day out. So it really can't be any more complicated than clicking one button in the IDE or typing one command at the prompt in order to run the tests you want. Some IDEs can even run the unit tests continually in the background.

It's important to maintain this environment where testing is easy: don't introduce a test that breaks the automatic model by requiring manual steps for that test to pass. Whatever resources the test requires (database, network connections, and so on), make the initialization of those resources an automatic part of the test itself. Don't forget to use the `SetUp` and `TearDown` methods when appropriate, as discussed in Chapter 3. Mock objects, as described in Chapter 6, can help insulate you from changes in the real environment if needed.

But you're not the only one running tests. Somewhere a machine should be running all the unit tests for all checked-in code continuously. This automatic, unattended check acts as a "backstop," in that a safety mechanism to ensure that whatever is checked in hasn't broken any tests, anywhere. In an ideal world, this wouldn't be necessary because you could count on every individual developer to run all the necessary tests themselves.

But this isn't an ideal world. Maybe an individual didn't run some necessary test in a remote corner of the project. Perhaps they have some code on their own machine that makes it all work, but they haven't committed that code to the source control system. Even though the tests work on their own machine, those same tests fail everywhere else. For this reason, it is critical that the automated build run *all* of the tests, including those sectioned off by `Category` and `Platform` attributes. If your project is a multiplatform .NET application, this means having multiple automated build machines for each target platform: one for Windows on x86 with Microsoft .NET, one for Linux on AMD64 with Mono, one for Mac OS on PowerPC with Mono, and so on. Note that this includes virtual machines as well.

You may want to investigate systems such as CruiseControl.NET[1] and other open source products that manage continuous building and testing.

Automatic Checking

Finally, by "automatic" we mean that the test must determine for itself whether it passed or failed. Having a person (you or some other hapless victim) read through the test output and determine whether the code is working is a recipe for project failure. Also, in the interests of speed, note that any test that spews tons of console I/O (via `Console.WriteLine`, `log4net`, or something similar) will slow down the unit tests—sometimes dramatically. We want unit tests to be silent, self-contained, and fast.

It's an important feature of consistent regression to have the tests check the results for themselves. We humans aren't very good at those repetitive tasks. We'll make mistakes in the checking and waste time investigating a bug that may not exist or not catch a new bug that will go on to cause additional damage. The computer will not make these inconsistent mistakes; a properly written unit test will check the same thing every time it's run with perfect consistency. Besides, we've got more important things to do—remember the project?

This idea of having the tests run by themselves and check themselves is critical, because it means you don't have to *think* about it—it just happens as part of the project. Testing can then fulfill its role as a major component of our project's safety net. (Version control and automation are the other two major components of the "safety net.") Tests are there to catch you when you fall, but they're not in your way.

You'll need all your concentration as you cross today's high wire.

---

[1] http://ccnet.thoughtworks.com

7.2 Thorough

A [T] RIP

Good unit tests are thorough; they test everything that's likely to break. But just how thorough?

At one extreme, you can aim to test every line of code, every possible branch the code might take, every exception it throws, and so on. At the other extreme, you test just the most likely candidates—boundary conditions, missing and malformed data, and so on. It's a question of judgment, based on the needs of your project.

If you want to aim for more complete coverage, then you may want to invest in a code coverage tool to help. For instance, NCover, which you can download from `http://ncover.org`,[2] produces XML files that describe the lines of code executed. You can use a couple of tools to visualize and explore that coverage data:

- NCoverExplorer[3] is available as an independent tool or as part of the TestDriven.NET extension to Visual Studio .NET.

- CruiseControl.NET comes with an XSL file for transforming the NCover XML into some really cool-looking HTML.

- SharpDevelop 2.1 (and newer) has NCover integration that will allow you to browse a tree view of classes and methods. It also has as an option to highlight lines of code in the IDE that were not covered by the unit tests.

These tools can help you determine how much of the code under test is actually being exercised, as well as help you pinpoint what's *not* being exercised so you can focus your testing efforts. Note that line-based coverage is not a panacea: you can have a very high percentage of line-based coverage but still have holes in the branch coverage. Code analysis tools and mutation testers can help close this gap, which we'll discuss in this chapter and in Chapter 8.

---

[2]As of this writing, NCover does not work with Mono because of the way it hooks into Microsoft-specific portions of the CLR.

[3]`http://kiwidude.com/blog`

It's important to realize that bugs are not evenly distributed throughout the source code. Instead, they tend to clump together in problematic areas (for an interesting story along these lines, see the sidebar on the following page).

This phenomenon leads to the well-known battle cry of "Don't patch it, rewrite it." Often, it can be cheaper and less painful to throw out a piece of code you've written that has a clump of bugs and rewrite it from scratch. Nothing can improve code quite like a good old-fashioned disk crash.

But because it's usually more fun to write new code rather than refactor existing code, be careful with wholesale rewriting—especially if it's someone else's code. Rather than throw it out, first try to refactor existing code to make it more unit testable. Then if that's not working, you can go ahead and succumb to the sweet siren song of coding from scratch.

Either way, refactoring or rewriting will be safer to do; you'll have a set of unit tests that can confirm the code works as it should.

7.3 Repeatable

Just as every test should be independent from every other test, the tests must be independent of the environment as well. The goal remains that every test should be able to run over and over again, in any order, *and produce the same results.* This means tests cannot rely on anything in the external environment that isn't under our direct control. That includes obvious external entities such as databases, system time, and network conditions but also perhaps less obvious dependents such as global variables. Any global state (in false singletons or otherwise) really isn't under our direct control— it only seems like it is.

A T **R** IP

Something, somewhere, when you least expect it, will alter that global state, and you'll end up spending a lot of quality time in the debugger trying to discover how the code got you into that state. That's the kind of frustration you just don't need.

Reported Bugs vs. Unit Test Coverage

We had a client recently who didn't quite believe in the power of unit tests. A few members of the team were very good and disciplined at writing unit tests for their own modules, many were somewhat sporadic about it, and a few refused to be bothered with unit tests at all.

As part of the hourly build process, we whipped up a simple Ruby script that performed a quick and dirty analysis of test coverage; it tallied up the ratio of test code asserts to production code methods for each module. Well-tested methods may have three, four, or more tests each; untested methods will have none at all. This analysis ran with every build and produced a bar graph, ranking the most-tested modules at the top and the untested modules at the bottom.

After a few weeks of gathering figures, we showed the bar graph to the project manager, without initial explanation. He was very surprised to see all the "problem modules" lumped together at the bottom— he thought we had somehow produced this graph based on bug reports from QA and customer support. Indeed, the modules at the top of the graph (well-tested) were nearly unknown to him; few, if any, problems had ever been reported against them. But the clump of modules at the bottom (that had no unit tests) were *very* well known to him, the support managers, and the local drugstore that had resorted to stocking extra-large supplies of antacid.

The results were nearly linear: the more unit tested the code, the fewer the problems.

Use mock objects as necessary to isolate the item under test and keep it independent from the environment. If you are forced to use some element from the real world (a database, perhaps), make sure you won't get interference from any other developer. Each developer needs their own "sandbox" to play in, whether that's their own database instance or their own web server on some nonstandard port.

Without repeatability, you might be in for some surprises at the worst possible moments. You can't afford to waste time chasing down phantom problems.

Each test should produce the same results every time. If it doesn't, that's a signal that there's a *real* bug in the implementation or the test code and its related `SetUp` and `Tear-Down` methods.

7.4 Independent

Tests need to be kept neat and tidy, which means keeping $A\ TR\ \boxed{I}\ P$ them tightly focused and independent from the environment and each other (remember, other developers may be running these same individual tests concurrently in separate threads).

When writing tests, make sure you are testing only one thing at a time.

Now that doesn't mean you should use only one assert in a test but that a test method should test only what the name implies—the same as regular methods in production code. If that means stitching a few methods together to accomplish the test, then so be it. Sometimes an entire test method might test only one small aspect of a complex piece of functionality— you may need multiple test methods to exercise the functionality thoroughly.

At any rate, you want to achieve a traceable correspondence between potential bugs and test code. In other words, when a test fails, it should be obvious where in the code the underlying bug exists without looking at the test code itself. The name of the test should tell us all we need to know. Otherwise, we've got to go hunting for it, and that will just waste our time.

Independent also means that no test relies on any other test; we should be able to run any individual test at any time and in any order. We *really* don't want to have to rely on any other test having run first, especially since the ordering will vary between the different test runners.

We've shown mechanisms to help you do this: the per-test setup and teardown methods and the per-fixture setup and teardown methods. Use these methods to ensure that every test gets a fresh start—and doesn't impact any test that might run next.

Remember, we aren't guaranteed that NUnit tests will run in any particular order, and as we start combining tests in ever-increasing numbers, we really can't afford to carry ordering dependencies along with us.

John Donne may have been right about people but not about unit tests: every test *should be* an island.

7.5 Professional

A TRI **P**

The code we write for a unit test is real; some may argue it's even more real than the code we ship to customers. This means it must be written and maintained to the same professional standards as production code. All the usual rules of good design—maintaining encapsulation, honoring the Don't Repeat Yourself principle [HT00], lowering coupling, and so on—must be followed in test code just as in production code.

It's easy to fall into the trap of writing very linear test code, that is, code that just plods along doing the same thing over and over again, using the same lines of code over and over again, with nary a function or object in sight. That's a bad thing. Test code must be written in the same manner as real code. That means we need to pull out common, repeated bits of code and put that functionality in a method instead so it can be called from several different places.

You may find you accumulate several related test methods that should be encapsulated in a class. Don't fight it!

Go ahead and create a new class, even if it's only ever used for testing. That's not only OK, it's encouraged. Test code is real code. In some cases, you may even need to create a larger framework or create a data-driven testing facility (remember the simple file reader for LargestTest on page 63?).

Don't waste time testing aspects that won't help you. Remember, you don't want to create tests just for the sake of creating tests. Test code must be thorough in that it must test everything interesting about a behavior that might break. If it's not likely to contain a bug, don't bother testing it. That means usually you shouldn't waste time testing things like simple property accessors:

```
public Money Balance
{
  get { return balance; }
}
```

Frankly, there's just not much here to go wrong that the compiler can't catch. Testing methods such as these is just a waste of time. However, if the property is doing some work along the way, then suddenly it becomes interesting—and we will want to test it:

```
public Money Balance
{
  get
  {
    return posted.GetBalance() -
        unposted.GetDebits() +
        unposted.GetCredits();
  }
}
```

That's probably worth testing.

Finally, expect that, in the end, there will be at least as much test code written as there will be production code. Yup, you read that right. If you have 20,000 lines of code in your project, then it would be reasonable to expect that there would be about 20,000 lines or more of unit test code to exercise it. That's a lot of test code, which is partly why it needs to be kept tidy, well-designed, and well-factored, just as professional as the production code.

7.6 Testing the Tests

Our plans so far have one major conceptual weakness. Testing code to make sure it works is a great idea, but we have to write code to perform the tests. What happens when there are bugs in our test code? Does that mean we have to write test code to test the tests that test the code? Where will it all end?

Fortunately, we don't need to go to that extreme. We can do two things to help ensure that the test code is correct:

- Improve tests when fixing bugs.
- Prove tests by introducing bugs.

How to Fix a Bug

The steps we take when fixing a bug are important to unit testing. Many times, an existing test will expose a bug in the code, and we can then simply fix the code and watch the vigilant test pass.

When a bug is found "in the wild" and reported, that means there's a hole in the safety net—a missing test. This is an opportunity to close the hole and make sure that this particular bug never escapes into the wild again. All it takes is four simple steps:

1. Identify the bug, or bugs, that caused the errant behavior.
2. Write a test that fails, for each individual bug, to prove the bug exists. Sometimes a bit of refactoring may need to happen in the method or class that contains the bug so that unit-level tests can be written more easily.
3. Fix the code such that the test now passes.
4. Verify that *all* tests still pass (that is, that you didn't break anything else as a result of the fix).

This simple mechanism of applying real-world feedback to help improve the tests is effective. Over time, you can expect that your test coverage will steadily increase and the number of bugs that escape into the wild from existing code will decrease.

Of course, as you write new code, you'll undoubtedly introduce new bugs, and new classes of bugs, that aren't being caught by the tests. But when fixing any bug, ask yourself this key question:

> **Could this same kind of problem happen anywhere else?**

Then it doesn't matter whether you're fixing a bug in an older feature or a new feature; either way, apply what you've just learned to the *whole* project.

Encode your newfound knowledge in all the unit tests that are appropriate, and you've done more than fix just one bug. You've caught a whole class of bugs and potentially found an opportunity to refactor similar code into one place for easier testing, maintenance, and enhancement.

Looking for Mr. Red Bar

It can be easy to write a test that has a bug whereby the test will always pass, even when there's a real bug in the implementation code. This can come up when a code review, automated or otherwise, reveals a real bug in code that is already being unit tested. Either the tests for that behavior aren't covering all the necessary lines and branch possibilities or the tests have a bug. It happens to the best of us, especially when first learning how to unit test or coding solo.

If we're not sure that a test is written correctly, the easiest thing to do is to "spring the trap": cause the production code to exhibit the very bug we're trying to detect, and verify that the test fails as expected. This is one of the only times we'll want to evoke a "red bar" in the NUnit GUI on purpose.

For instance, suppose we have a test method that adds a customer account to the database and then tries to find it, something like the code in Figure 7.1 on the following page. Perhaps we're not certain that the "finding" part is really working—it might be reporting success even if the record wasn't added correctly.

```
[Test]
public void Add()
{
  // Create a new account object
  Account account = new Account();
  // Populate with our test person
  acct.SetPerson(MATT);
  // Add it to the database
  repository.Save(account);
  // Should find it
  Assert.That(repository.findByPersonId(MATT.Id),
          Is.NotNull);
}
```

Figure 7.1: Test adding a person to a database

So maybe we'll go into the Save() method for repository and short-circuit it: just return instead of actually adding the record to the underlying storage mechanism encapsulated by the repository. Now we should see the assertion fail, because the record has not been added.

But wait, you may cry, what about a leftover record from a previous test run? Won't that be in the repository? No, it won't, for several reasons:

- We may not really be testing against a repository that encapsulates a live database. The code exercised by the previous test case lies between the add method shown and the underlying storage mechanism. That underlying storage mechanism may just be a Dictionary collection whose data is not held persistently in between runs. When implementing the Repository pattern [Fow03], it is common to have an in-memory variety for testing and data aggregation purposes.

- Tests are independent. All tests can be run in any order and do not depend on each other, so even if a real database is part of this test (directly or indirectly), the setup and teardown must ensure that we get a "clean sandbox" to play in. The previous attempt to spring the trap can help prove that this is true. In this case, we would re-create the in-memory repository each time in the setup method in this test's fixture class.

The Extreme Programming folks claim that their disciplined practice of test-first development avoids the problem of poor tests that don't fail when they should. In test-first development, you only ever write code to fix a failing test. As soon as the test passes, then you know that the code you just added fixed it. This puts you in the position where you always know with absolute certainty that the code you introduced fixes the failing test that caused you to write the code in the first place.

But there's many a slip 'twixt the cup and the lip, and although test-first development does improve the situation dramatically, there will still be opportunities to be misled by coincidences. The practice of pair programming further reduces the chance of these kinds of slip-ups, but you may not always have someone to pair with. Leaning on the compiler and code analysis tools can help, but neither is a panacea. For those occasions, you can satisfy any lingering doubts by deliberately "springing the trap" to make sure all is as you expect.

Finally, remember to write tests that are A TRIP (Automatic, Thorough, Repeatable, Independent, Professional), keep adding to your unit tests as new bugs and types of bugs are discovered, and check to make sure your tests really do find the bugs they target.

Then sit back and watch problems on your project disappear like magic.

Chapter 8

Testing on a Project

Up to now we've talked about testing as an individual, solitary exercise. But of course in the real world, you'll likely have teammates to work with. You'll all be unit testing together, and that brings up a couple of issues.

8.1 Where to Put Test Code

On a small, one-person project, the location of test code and encapsulation of the production code may not be very important, but on larger projects it can become a critical issue. We can structure our production and test code in several ways that we'll look at here.

In general, we don't want to break any encapsulation for the sake of testing (or as Mom used to say, "Don't expose your privates!"). Most of the time, we should be able to test a class by exercising its public methods. If there is significant functionality that is hidden behind private or protected access, that might be a warning sign that there's another class in there struggling to get out. When push comes to shove, however, it's probably better to break encapsulation with working, tested code than it is to have good encapsulation of untested, potentially buggy code.

Same Directory

Suppose we are writing a class named like this:

```
PragProg.Wibble.Account
```

with a corresponding test like so:

```
PragProg.Wibble.AccountTest
```

The first and easiest method of structuring test code is to simply include it right in the same project and assembly alongside the production code.

This has the advantage that AccountTest can access internal and protected internal member variables and methods of Account. But the disadvantage is that the test code is lying around, cluttering up the production code directory. This may or may not be a problem depending on the method of creating a release to ship to customers.

Most of the time, it's enough of a problem that we prefer one of the other solutions. But for small projects, this might be sufficient.

Separate Assemblies

The next option is to create our tests in a separate assembly from the production code. This has the advantage of keeping a clean separation between code that we ship and code for testing.

The disadvantage is that now the test code is in a different assembly; we won't be able to access internal or protected internal members unless our test code uses a subclass of the production code that exposes the necessary members. For instance, suppose the class we want to test looks like this:

```
namespace FacilitiesManagment
{
  public class Pool
  {
    protected Date lastCleaned;
    public void xxx, xx
    {
      xxx xxx xxx;
    }
    ...
  }
}
```

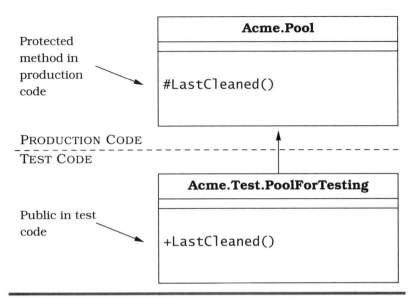

Figure 8.1: SUBCLASSES EXPOSE METHODS FOR TESTING

We need to get at that nonpublic bit of data that tells us when the pool was last cleaned for testing, but there's no public accessor for it. (If there were, the pool association would probably sue us; they don't like to make that information public.) So, we make a subclass that exposes it just for testing:

```
using FacilitiesManagment;
namespace FacilitiesManagmentTesting
{
  public class PoolForTesting : Pool
  {
    public DateTime LastCleaned
    {
      get { return lastCleaned; }
    }
  }
}
```

We then use PoolForTesting in the test code instead of using Pool directly (see Figure 8.1). In fact, we could make this class internal to the test assembly (to ensure that we don't get sued).

Whatever convention the team decides to adopt, make sure it does so consistently. You cannot have some of the tests in the system set up one way and other tests elsewhere set up a different way. Pick a style that looks like it will work in your environment, and stick with it for all of the system's unit tests.

8.2 Where to Put NUnit

One issue that comes up on real projects is how to distribute NUnit itself.

You could install the latest version of NUnit on each workstation where the tests will be built and run (including the automated build machine). NUnit would need to be installed into the same directory on all current and future workstations so that the code can reference that specific `nunit.framework.dll` assembly, and not some random one that happens to be in the global assembly cache (GAC) or elsewhere. This is all actually more difficult than it sounds, especially if you eventually need to upgrade to newer versions of NUnit; Visual Studio exhibits a variety of little bugs when resolving assembly references.

Instead, you should distribute NUnit via your version control system. Many .NET and Java projects define both a `src/` directory and a `lib/` directory. The `src/` directory contains the source code to the project, and the `lib/` directory contains precompiled components (usually third-party).

In this context, you'd have a `lib/nunit/` directory that contains the NUnit binary distribution. Your projects and build files should reference `nunit.framework.dll` in this directory, and developers should run the `nunit.exe` GUI from this directory via a shortcut.

Now keeping developers' versions of NUnit synchronized is easy, as is deploying any upgrades or customizations. It keeps the environment consistent, freeing up time that would otherwise be spent on figuring out mismatched NUnit version issues (which usually manifest themselves in odd ways). You may want to discourage developers from installing NUnit on their workstations to reduce confusion. If they do, keep an eye out for changes in the project or build files that reference NUnit assemblies other than those in the project's `lib/nunit/` directory.

Obfuscation and Packaging

Matt tells the following story about packaging, obfuscation, and manual maintenance:

"Recently I worked on a project that used a code obfuscation program. They packaged their unit tests in the same assembly as their production code, but the unit tests were #if'd out in the release build. Anytime a developer added a new test file, they had to remember to add the #if or risk violating the obfuscation policy. Or, did they?

"Putting the tests into the assembly was reducing the effective design feedback of their packaging (which had major issues), so I proposed to extract the unit tests into a separate assembly so the design issues could be made more obvious. They said this was impossible because the unit tests were testing classes marked internal, and thus the tests had to be inside the same assembly as the production code.

"I was curious why these classes had to be internal, and this turned up an amusing (albeit embarrassing) misunderstanding: the team thought that in order for the obfuscater to work properly, classes had to be marked as internal. That is, they thought public classes wouldn't be obfuscated in name or in code.

"This was a mistake, as I learned after reading the manual. This particular obfuscater didn't really care, and I was able to configure it to obfuscate everything just fine. One of the neat tricks that came out of this was that this obfuscation product was able to take several assemblies that referenced each other, combine them into one binary, and prune out unused methods and code.

"Because the unit tests weren't referenced directly in any of the application code, they were pruned out automatically by the obfuscation product. The manual #if statements they kept using could simply be removed. This also opened the door to making those internal classes public; the unit tests could then be extracted into a separate assembly, and design feedback could be obtained and acted upon appropriately."

8.3 Test Courtesy

The biggest difference between testing by yourself and testing with others lies in synchronizing working tests and code.

When working with other members of a team, you will be using some sort of version control system, such as Subversion, CVS, or (for the more masochistic among us) Visual Source-Safe. (If you aren't familiar with version control or want some assistance in getting it set up and working correctly, please see [TH03].)

In a team environment (and even in a personal environment), you should make sure that when you check in code (or otherwise make it available to everyone), it has complete unit tests and passes all of them. In fact, every test in the whole system should continue to pass with your new code.

The rule is simple: as soon as anyone else can access your code, all tests everywhere need to pass. Since you should usually work in fairly close synchronization with the rest of the team and the version control system, this boils down to "All tests pass all the time."

Many teams institute policies to help "remind" developers of the consequences of breaking the build or breaking the tests. These policies might begin by listing potential infractions involving code that you have checked in (or otherwise made available to other developers):

- Incomplete code (such as checking in only one class file but forgetting to check in other files it may depend upon)

- Code that doesn't compile

- Code that compiles but breaks existing code such that existing code no longer compiles

- Code without corresponding unit tests

- Code with failing unit tests

- Code that passes its own tests but causes other tests elsewhere in the system to fail

If found guilty of any of these heinous crimes, you may be sentenced to providing donuts, soda, or frozen margaritas to the whole team, or maybe you'll have to play nursemaid to the build machine or some other token, menial task.

A little lighthearted law enforcement usually provides enough motivation against careless accidents. But what happens if you have to make an incompatible change to the code or if you make a change that *does* cause other tests to fail elsewhere in the system?

The precise answer depends on the methodology and process you're using on the project, but somehow you need to coordinate your changes with the folks who are responsible for the other pieces of code—which may well be you! The idea is to make all the necessary changes at once so the rest of the team sees a coherent picture (that actually works) instead of a fragmented nonfunctional "work in progress." (For more information about how to use version control to set up experimental developer branches, see [TH03].)

Sometimes the real world is not so willing, and it might take a few hours or even a few days to work out all the incompatible bits and pieces, during which time the build is broken. If it can't be helped, then make sure it is well-communicated. Make sure everyone knows that the build will be broken for the requisite amount of time so that everyone can plan around it as needed. If you're not involved, maybe it would be a good time to take your car in for an oil change or slip off to the beach for a day or two. If you are involved, get it done quickly so everyone else can come back from the beach and get to work!

8.4 Test Frequency

How often should you run unit tests? It depends on what you're doing and your personal habits, but here are some general guidelines that we find helpful. You want to perform enough testing to make sure you're catching everything you need to catch but not so much testing that it interferes with producing production code.

When you:

Write a new method.

Compile and run local unit tests.

Fix a bug.

Write and run tests[1] that demonstrate the bug; fix the bug and rerun all the unit tests.

Compile successfully after making code modification.

Run local unit tests.

Check in a file to version control.

Run all module or system unit tests.

In addition to those event-driven tests, you need to be testing continuously. A dedicated machine should be running a full build and test, from scratch, automatically throughout the day (either periodically or on check-in to version control).

Note that for larger projects you might not be able to compile and test the whole system in less than a few hours. You may be able to run a full build and test only overnight. For even larger projects, it may have to be every couple of days—and that's a shame, because the longer the time between automatic builds, the longer the "feedback gap" between the creation of a problem and its identification.

The reason to have a more or less continuous build is so it can identify any problems quickly. You don't want to have to wait for another developer to stumble upon a build problem if you can help it. Having a build machine act as a constant developer increases the odds that *it* will find a problem, instead of a real developer.

When the build machine does find a problem, then the whole team can be alerted to the fact that it's not safe to get any new code just yet and can continue working with what they have. That's better than getting stuck in a situation where you've gotten fresh code that doesn't work.

---

[1]Sometimes, a single bug may have several root causes, each of which need a focused unit test.

For more information on setting up automatic build and testing systems, nightly and continuous builds, and automation in general, please see [Cla04].

8.5 Tests and Legacy Code

So far, we've talked about performing unit tests in the context of new code. But we haven't said what to do if your project has a lot of code already—code that *doesn't* have unit tests.

It all depends on what kind of state that code is in. If it's reasonably well-factored and modular so that you can get at all of the individual pieces you need to, then you can add unit tests fairly easily. If, on the other hand, it's just a "big ball of mud" all tangled together, then it might be close to impossible to test without substantial rewriting. Most older projects aren't perfectly factored but are usually modular enough that you can add unit tests.

For new code you write, you'll obviously write unit tests as well. This may mean you'll have to expose or break out parts of the existing system or create mock objects in order to test your new functionality.

For existing code, you might choose to add unit tests methodically for everything that is testable. But that's not very pragmatic. It's better to add tests for the most broken stuff first so you can realize a better return on investment of effort.

An important aspect of unit tests in this environment is to prevent backsliding; in other words, we want to avoid the death spiral where maintenance fixes and enhancements cause bugs in existing features. We use NUnit unit tests as *regression* tests during normal new code development (to make sure new code doesn't break anything that had been working), but regression testing is even more important when dealing with legacy code.

And it doesn't have to cover the entire legacy code base, just the painful parts. Consider the following true story from a pragmatic developer (the team in question happened to be using Java and JUnit for this particular project, but they could just as easily have been using C#, Cobol, C++, Ruby, or any other programming language):

Regression Tests Save the Day

"Tibbert Enterprises[2] ships multiple applications, all of which are based on a common lower-level library that is used to access the object database.

"One day I overheard some application developers talking about a persistent problem they were having. In the product's lower-level interface, you can look up objects using the object name, which includes a path to the object. Since the application has several layers between it and the lower-level code, and the lower-level code has several more layers to reach the object database, it takes a while to isolate a problem when the application breaks.

"And the application broke. After half the application team spent an entire day tracking down the bug, they discovered the bug was in the lower-level code that accessed the database. If you had a space in the name, the application died a violent, messy death. After isolating the lower-level code related to the database access, they presented the bug to the owner of the code, along with a fix. He thanked them, incorporated their fix, and committed the fixed code into the repository.

"But the next day, the application died. Once again, a team of application developers tracked it down. It took only half a day this time (because they recognized the code paths by now), and the bug was in the same place. This time, it was a space in the path to the object that was failing, instead of a space in the name itself. Apparently, while integrating the fix, the developer had introduced a new bug. Once again, they tracked it down and presented him with a fix. It's day three, and the application is failing again! Apparently the developer in question reintroduced the original bug.

---

[2]Not its real name.

"The application manager and I sat down and figured out that the equivalent of nearly two months of effort had been spent on this one issue over the course of one week by his team alone (and this likely affected other teams throughout the company). We then developed JUnit tests that tested the lower-level API calls that the application product was using and added tests for database access using spaces in both the object name and in the path. We put the product under the control of our continuous-build-and-test program (using Cruise-Control) so that the unit tests were run automatically every time code got committed back to the repository.

"Sure enough, the following week, the test failed on two successive days at the hands of the original developer. He actually came to my office, shook my hand, and thanked me when he got the automatic notification that the tests had failed.

"You see, without the JUnit test, the bad code made it out to the entire company during the nightly builds. But with our continuous build and test, he (and his manager and tester) saw the failure at once, and he was able to fix it immediately before anyone else in the company used the code. In fact, this test has failed half a dozen times since then. But it gets caught, so it's not a big deal anymore. The product is now stable because of these tests.

"We now have a rule that any issue that pops up twice must have a JUnit test by the end of the week."

In this story, Tibbert Enterprises isn't using unit testing to prove things work so much as it is using unit testing to inoculate against known issues. As the company slowly catches up, it'll eventually expand to cover the entire product with unit tests, not just the most broken parts.

When you come into a shop with no automated tests of any kind, this seems to be an effective approach. Remember, the only way to eat an elephant is one bite at a time.

8.6 Tests and Code Reviews

Teams that enjoy success often hold code reviews. This can be an informal affair where a senior person just gives a quick look at the code. Or perhaps two people are working on the code together, using Extreme Programming's *pair programming* practice.

Many teams also use free automated code analysis tools such as gendarme[3] or FxCop,[4] configured only to check for the rules that matter to the project at hand. Some teams even go the extra step to write custom rules for the code analysis tools and to include code analysis in their automated build, increasing the effectiveness of their projects' safety net.

There are also automated tools, known as *mutators*, that can help find holes in the test coverage. One of these is called Nester.[5] Nester mutates your code in various ways that inverses the logic of branch statements, one change at a time, and reruns the tests to see whether they fail. If the tests still pass after one of these mutations, there's a hole in the branch coverage.

This is akin to the protocol "fuzzing" tools that some teams use to make sure networking products fail correctly when given bad data. You can also do these mutations manually every once in awhile; change a logical and (&&) to a logical or (||), make a bet with your co-worker that the tests will pass or fail, and rerun the tests. Whoever said you can't get rich by unit testing?

However you perform code reviews (and we suggest that you do), make the test code an integral part of the review process. Since test code is held up to the same high standards as production code, it should be reviewed as well.

In fact, it can sometimes be helpful to expand on the idea of "test-first design" to include both writing and *reviewing* test code before writing production code.

---

[3]http://www.mono-project.com/gendarme
[4]http://blogs.msdn.com/fxcop
[5]Nester's website is at nester.sourceforge.net. Nester is based on the tool Jester for Java.

That is, code and review in this order:

1. Write test cases and/or test code.

2. Review test cases and/or test code for usability and readability.

3. Revise test cases and/or test code per review.

4. Write production code that passes the tests.

5. Review production and test code.

6. Revise test and production code per review.

Reviews of the test code are incredibly useful. Not only can reviews sometimes be more effective than testing at finding bugs in the first place, but by having everyone involved in reviews you can improve team communication. People on the team get to see how others do testing, see what the team's conventions are, and help keep everyone honest. Since unit test code also serves as documentation, having more than one pair of eyes on them helps ensure the code expresses its intention clearly to more than one person.

You can use the checklists on page 209 of this book to help identify possible test cases in reviews. But don't go overboard testing things that aren't likely to break, and don't repeat essentially similar tests over and over just for the sake of testing.

Finally, you may want to keep track of common problems that come up again and again. These might be areas where more training might be needed, an automated code analysis tool can be enhanced, or perhaps something else that should be added to your standard review checklist.

For example, at a client's site several years ago, we discovered that many of the developers misunderstood exception handling. The code base was full of fragments similar to the following:

```
try
{
    DatabaseConnection dbc = new DatabaseConnection();
    InsertNewRecord(dbc, record);
    dbc.Close();
}
catch (Exception) {}
```

> ### Delusional Exception Handling
>
> Matt adds this story:
>
> "I was working on a project where the company's CTO littered the code with empty `catch` statements. When running a runtime analysis tool, I noticed that several dozen exceptions were being thrown and handled. Upon further inspection, I saw a piece of code that would almost always fail because it was— wait for it—dividing by a value that was zero most of the time.
>
> "The team found this appalling, so we spent a day cleaning up all the empty `catch`-all statements. The CTO was upset because the product was now more visibly unstable. He demanded the team put the bad exception handling back in. The team refused—the bugs and broken functionality were always present; the difference was we could *see* how bad it was. By fixing the root of the problem, the product was in better shape when it was released and went on to win awards."

That is to say, they simply ignored any exceptions that might have occurred. Not only did this result in random missing records, but the system leaked database connections as well—any error that came up would cause the `Close` to be skipped.

We added this to the list of known, typical problems to be checked during reviews. As code was reviewed, any of these infamous `catch` statements that were discovered were first identified, then proper unit tests were put in place to force various error conditions (the "E" in Right BICEP), and the code was fixed to either propagate or handle the exception. System stability increased tremendously as a result of this simple process. For reference, the minimal fix is to close (or dispose) resources in a `finally` clause. That way, they'll be cleaned up when control flow leaves the `try` block—whether an exception is thrown or not.

```
try
{
    DatabaseConnection dbc = new DatabaseConnection();
    InsertNewRecord(dbc, record);
}
finally
{
    dbc.Close();
}
```

Another way to express this is with the using statement:

```
using (DatabaseConnection dbc = new DatabaseConnection())
{
    InsertNewRecord(dbc, record);
}
```

The code generated by the C# compiler actually includes a try/finally block like the previous example. Either way works, so use whatever you and your team is comfortable with. Just make sure to be consistent to make code reviews go more smoothly.

Chapter 9

Design Issues

So far we have discussed unit testing because it helps you understand and verify the functional, operational characteristics of your code. But unit testing offers several opportunities to improve the design and architecture of your code as well.

In this chapter, we'll take a look at the following design-level issues:

- Separating concerns better by designing for testability

- Clarifying design by defining class invariants

- Improving interfaces with test-driven design

- Establishing and localizing validation responsibilities

9.1 Designing for Testability

The separation of concerns is probably the single most important concept in software design and implementation. It's the catchall phrase that encompasses encapsulation, orthogonality, coupling, and all those other computer science terms that boil down to "write shy code" [HT00].

We can keep your code well-factored (that is, "shy") and easier to maintain by explicitly designing code to be testable. For example, suppose we are writing a method that will sleep until the top of the next hour.

We've got a bunch of calculations and then a `Sleep()`:

```
public void SleepUntilNextHour() {
  int howlong;
  xx xxxx x xxxx xx xx xxx;
  // Calculate how long to wait...
  x x xx xxx xxx x x xx
  xx xxxx x xxxx xx xx xxx;
  Thread.Sleep(howlong);
  return;
}
```

How will we test that? Wait around for an hour? Set a timer, call the method, wait for the method to return, check the timer, handle the cases when the method doesn't get called when it should—this is starting to get pretty messy. We saw something similar back in Chapter 6, but this issue is important enough to revisit. Once again, we'll refactor the method in order to make testing easier.

Instead of combining the calculation of how many milliseconds to sleep with the `Sleep()` method itself, split them up:

```
public void SleepUntilNextHour() {
  int howlong = MilliSecondsToNextHour(DateTime.Now);
  Thread.Sleep(howlong);
  return;
}
```

What's likely to break? The system's `Sleep` call? Or our code that calculates the amount of time to wait? It's probably a fair bet to say that .NET's `Thread.Sleep()` works as advertised (even if it doesn't, our rule is to always suspect our own code first; see the tip *Select Isn't Broken* in [HT00]). So for now, we need to test only that the number of milliseconds is calculated correctly, and what might have been a hairy test with timers and all sorts of logic (not to mention an hour's wait) can be expressed very simply like this:

```
Assert.AreEqual(10000, MilliSecondsToNextHour(DATE_1));
```

If we're confident that `MilliSecondsToNextHour()` works to our satisfaction, then the odds are that `SleepUntilNextHour()` will be reliable as well—if it is not, then at least we know that the problem must be related to the sleep itself, not to the numerical calculation. We might even be able to reuse the `MilliSecondsToNextHour()` method in some other context.

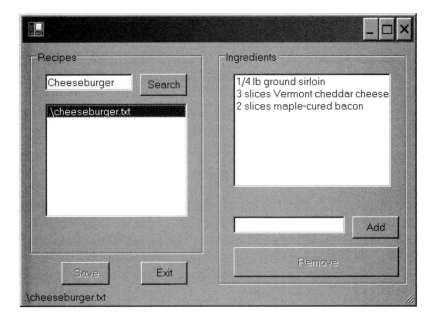

Figure 9.1: RECIPES GUI SCREEN

This is what we mean when we claim we can improve the design of code by making it easier to test. By changing code so that we can get in there and test it, we'll end up with a cleaner design that's easier to extend and maintain as well as test.

But instead of boring you with examples and techniques, all you really need to do is remember this one fundamental question when writing code:

How are we going to test this?

If the answer is not obvious or if it looks like the test would be ugly or hard to write, then take that as a warning signal. Your design probably needs to be modified; change things around until the code is easy to test, and your design will end up being far better for the effort.

Figure 9.2: Original Recipes static class diagram

9.2 Refactoring for Testing

Let's look at a real-life example. Here are excerpts from a novice's first attempt at a recipe management system. The GUI, shown in Figure 9.1 on the previous page, is pretty straightforward. There's only one class, with GUI behavior and file I/O intermixed.

It reads and writes individual recipes to files, using a line-oriented format, somewhat like an INI or properties file:

```
NAME=Cheeseburger
INGREDIENTS=3
1/4 lb ground sirloin
3 slices Vermont cheddar cheese
2 slices maple-cured bacon
```

And the following shows the code in its entirety. As is, this is pretty hard to test. We have to run the whole program and operate the GUI to get at any part of it. All the file I/O and search routines access the widgets directly, so they are tightly coupled to the GUI code (see, for instance, lines 146, 161, 170, and 181). In fact, the UML diagram for this class, shown in Figure 9.2, is kind of embarrassing—it's just one big class! Unfortunately, this kind of code is commonplace in many C# projects because the designer-generated code created by most IDEs stealthily coerces programmers to add logic directly into the Form or Control class. Design-level tools for WinForms and ASP.NET are great tools—just be aware of these sinful temptations.

cheeseburger.txt

```
Line 1   using System;
    -    using System.Collections;
    -    using System.ComponentModel;
    -    using System.Drawing;
    5    using System.IO;
    -    using System.Windows.Forms;

    -    public class Recipes : Form
    -    {
    10     private Button exitButton = new Button();
    -      private StatusBar statusBar = new StatusBar();
    -      private GroupBox searchGroupBox = new GroupBox();
    -      private ListBox searchList = new ListBox();
    -      private GroupBox ingredientsGroupBox = new GroupBox();
    15     private ListBox ingredientsList = new ListBox();
    -      private Button removeButton = new Button();
    -      private TextBox ingredientsText = new TextBox();
    -      private Button saveButton = new Button();
    -      private Button addButton = new Button();
    20     private Button searchButton = new Button();
    -      private TextBox titleText = new TextBox();

    -      public Recipes()
    -      {
    25       InitializeComponent();
    -      }

    -      private void InitializeComponent()
    -      {
    30       exitButton.Location =
    -          new System.Drawing.Point(120, 232);
    -        exitButton.Size = new System.Drawing.Size(48, 24);
    -        exitButton.Text = "E&xit";
    -        exitButton.Click +=
    35         new System.EventHandler(exitButton_Click);

    -        statusBar.Location = new System.Drawing.Point(0, 261);
    -        statusBar.Size = new System.Drawing.Size(400, 16);

    40       searchGroupBox.Controls.Add(titleText);
    -        searchGroupBox.Controls.Add(searchList);
    -        searchGroupBox.Controls.Add(searchButton);
    -        searchGroupBox.Location = new System.Drawing.Point(8, 8);
    -        searchGroupBox.Size = new System.Drawing.Size(176, 216);
    45       searchGroupBox.TabStop = false;
    -        searchGroupBox.Text = "Recipes";

    -        searchList.Location = new System.Drawing.Point(16, 56);
    -        searchList.Size = new System.Drawing.Size(144, 147);
    50       searchList.SelectedIndexChanged +=
    -          new System.EventHandler(
    -            searchList_SelectedIndexChanged);

    -        searchButton.Location = new System.Drawing.Point(112, 24);
    55       searchButton.Size = new System.Drawing.Size(48, 20);
    -        searchButton.Text = "S&earch";
```

```
  -          searchButton.Click +=
  -            new System.EventHandler(searchButton_Click);
  -
 60          titleText.Location = new System.Drawing.Point(16, 24);
  -          titleText.Size = new System.Drawing.Size(88, 20);
  -
  -          ingredientsGroupBox.Controls.Add(ingredientsList);
  -          ingredientsGroupBox.Controls.Add(ingredientsText);
 65          ingredientsGroupBox.Controls.Add(addButton);
  -          ingredientsGroupBox.Controls.Add(removeButton);
  -          ingredientsGroupBox.Location = new System.Drawing.Point(200, 8);
  -          ingredientsGroupBox.Size = new System.Drawing.Size(192, 248);
  -          ingredientsGroupBox.TabStop = false;
 70          ingredientsGroupBox.Text = "Ingredients";
  -
  -          addButton.Location = new System.Drawing.Point(136, 176);
  -          addButton.Size = new System.Drawing.Size(48, 23);
  -          addButton.Text = "&Add";
 75          addButton.Click +=
  -            new System.EventHandler(addButton_Click);
  -
  -          ingredientsText.Location = new System.Drawing.Point(16, 176);
  -          ingredientsText.Size = new System.Drawing.Size(112, 20);
 80
  -          removeButton.Enabled = false;
  -          removeButton.Location = new System.Drawing.Point(16, 208);
  -          removeButton.Size = new System.Drawing.Size(168, 32);
  -          removeButton.Text = "&Remove";
 85          removeButton.Click +=
  -            new System.EventHandler(removeButton_Click);
  -
  -          ingredientsList.Location = new System.Drawing.Point(16, 24);
  -          ingredientsList.Size = new System.Drawing.Size(160, 134);
 90          ingredientsList.SelectedIndexChanged +=
  -            new System.EventHandler(
  -              ingredientsList_SelectedIndexChanged);
  -
  -          saveButton.Enabled = false;
 95          saveButton.Location = new System.Drawing.Point(40, 232);
  -          saveButton.Size = new System.Drawing.Size(48, 24);
  -          saveButton.Text = "&Save";
  -          saveButton.Click +=
  -            new System.EventHandler(saveButton_Click);
100
  -          AutoScaleBaseSize = new System.Drawing.Size(5, 13);
  -          ClientSize = new System.Drawing.Size(400, 277);
  -          Controls.Add(saveButton);
  -          Controls.Add(searchGroupBox);
105          Controls.Add(ingredientsGroupBox);
  -          Controls.Add(statusBar);
  -          Controls.Add(exitButton);
  -          ingredientsGroupBox.ResumeLayout(false);
  -          searchGroupBox.ResumeLayout(false);
110          ResumeLayout(false);
  -        }
  -
```

```
          [STAThread]
          static void Main()
115       {
            Directory.SetCurrentDirectory(@"../../recipes/");
            Application.Run(new Recipes());
          }

120       private void exitButton_Click(object sender,
                                        System.EventArgs e)
          {
            Application.Exit();
          }
125
          private void searchButton_Click(object sender,
                                          System.EventArgs e)
          {
            String toMatch = "*" + titleText.Text + "*";
130
            try
            {
              string [] matchingFiles = Directory.GetFiles(@".", toMatch);
              searchList.DataSource = matchingFiles;
135         }
            catch (Exception error)
            {
              statusBar.Text = error.Message;
            }
140       }

          private void
          searchList_SelectedIndexChanged(object sender,
                                          System.EventArgs e)
145       {
            string file = (string)searchList.SelectedItem;
            string line;
            char [] delim = new char[] { '=' };

150         statusBar.Text = file;

            using (StreamReader reader =
                     new StreamReader(file))
            {
155           while ((line = reader.ReadLine()) != null)
              {
                string [] tokens = line.Split(delim, 2);
                switch (tokens[0])
                {
160               case "NAME":
                    titleText.Text = tokens[1];
                    break;
                  case "INGREDIENTS":
                    try
165                 {
                      int count = Int32.Parse(tokens[1]);
                      ingredientsList.Items.Clear();
```

```
  -                   for (int i = 0; i < count; i++)
  -                   {
170                     ingredientsList.Items.Add(reader.ReadLine());
  -                   }
  -                 }
  -                 catch (Exception error)
  -                 {
175                   statusBar.Text = "Bad ingredient count: " +
  -                     error.Message;
  -                   return;
  -                 }
  -                 break;
180             default:
  -                 statusBar.Text = "Invalid recipe line: " + line;
  -                 return;
  -             }
  -           }
185       }
  -       saveButton.Enabled = false;
  -     }
  -
  -     private void removeButton_Click(object sender,
190                                     System.EventArgs e)
  -     {
  -       int index = ingredientsList.SelectedIndex;
  -       if (index >= 0)
  -       {
195         statusBar.Text = "Removed " +
  -           ingredientsList.SelectedItem;
  -         ingredientsList.Items.RemoveAt(index);
  -         saveButton.Enabled = true;
  -       }
200     }
  -
  -     private void addButton_Click(object sender,
  -                                  System.EventArgs e)
  -     {
205       string newIngredient = ingredientsText.Text;
  -       if (newIngredient.Length > 0)
  -       {
  -         ingredientsList.Items.Add(newIngredient);
  -         saveButton.Enabled = true;
210       }
  -     }
  -
  -     private void
  -     ingredientsList_SelectedIndexChanged(object sender,
215                                          System.EventArgs e)
  -     {
  -       int index = ingredientsList.SelectedIndex;
  -       if (index < 0)
  -       {
220         removeButton.Enabled = false;
  -       }
  -       else
```

```
          {
            removeButton.Text = "&Remove " +
225           ingredientsList.SelectedItem;
            removeButton.Enabled = true;
          }
        }

230     private void saveButton_Click(object sender,
                                        System.EventArgs e)
        {
          string fileName = titleText.Text + ".txt";
          ICollection items = ingredientsList.Items;
235       using (StreamWriter file =
                    new StreamWriter(fileName, false))
          {
            file.WriteLine("NAME={0}", titleText.Text);
            file.WriteLine("INGREDIENTS={0}", items.Count);
240         foreach (string line in items)
            {
              file.WriteLine(line);
            }
          }
245       statusBar.Text = "Saved " + fileName;
        }
      }
```

Recipes.cs

We clearly need to improve this code. Let's begin by making a
separate object to hold a recipe so that we can construct test
recipe data easily and toss it back and forth to the screen,
disk, network, or wherever. This is just a simple data holder,
with accessors for the data members:

```
Line 1  using System;
      using System.Collections.Generic;
      using System.Collections.ObjectModel;

5     public class Recipe
      {
        protected string name;
        protected List<string> ingredients;

10      public Recipe()
        {
          name = string.Empty;
          ingredients = new List<string>();
        }
15
        public Recipe(Recipe another)
        {
          name = another.name;
          ingredients = new List<string>(another.ingredients);
20      }
```

Recipe.cs

```
     public string Name
     {
       get { return name; }
25     set { name = value; }
     }

     public ReadOnlyCollection<string> Ingredients
     {
30     get
       {
         return
           new ReadOnlyCollection<string>(ingredients);
       }
35   }

     public void AddIngredient(string ingredient)
     {
       ingredients.Add(ingredient);
40   }
   }
```

Next, we need to pull the code out from the original Recipes class to save and load a file to disk.

To help separate file I/O from any other kind of I/O, we'll perform the file I/O in a helper class that uses Recipe. We want to take out all the GUI widget references from the original source code and use instance member variables instead:

```
Line 1  public class RecipeFile
   {
     public Recipe Load(Stream savedRecipe)
     {
5
       using (StreamReader reader = new StreamReader(savedRecipe))
       {
         string line;
         List<string> lines = new List<string>();
10       while ((line = reader.ReadLine()) != null)
         {
           lines.Add(line);
         }
15       return createRecipe(lines);
       }
     }

     public void Save(Stream savedRecipe, Recipe recipe)
20   {
       using (StreamWriter file = new StreamWriter(savedRecipe))
       {
         file.WriteLine("NAME={0}", recipe.Name);
         file.WriteLine(
25         "INGREDIENTS={0}",
           recipe.Ingredients.Count
         );
```

```
              foreach (string line in recipe.Ingredients)
30            {
                  file.WriteLine(line);
              }
          }
      }
35
      private Recipe createRecipe(ICollection<string> lines)
      {
        char[] delim = new char[] {'='};
        Recipe recipe = new Recipe();
40      foreach (string line in lines)
        {
          string[] tokens = line.Split(delim, 2);

          switch (tokens[0])
45        {
            case "TITLE":
            {
              recipe.Name = tokens[1];
              break;
50          }
            case "INGREDIENTS":
            {
              try
              {
55              int count = Int32.Parse(tokens[1]);
                for (int i = 0; i < count; i++)
                {
                    recipe.AddIngredient(line);
                }
60            }
              catch (IOException error)
              {
                throw new RecipeFormatException(
                  "Bad ingredient count: " + error.Message);
65            }
              break;
            }
          }
        }
70
      return recipe;
      }
  }
```

RecipeFile.cs

Now we're in a position where we can write a genuine test case that will test reading and writing to disk, without using any GUI code:

```
Line 1   using NUnit.Framework;
         using NUnit.Framework.SyntaxHelpers;
         using System;
         using System.Collections.Generic;
```

```
 5   using System.IO;

     [TestFixture]
     public class RecipeTest
     {
10     const string CHEESEBURGER = "Cheeseburger";
       const string SIRLOIN = "1/4 lb ground sirloin";
       const string CHEESE = "3 slices Vermont ched-
dar cheese";
       const string BACON = "2 slices maple-cured bacon";
       const string RECIPE_FILE_NAME = "recipe.save";
15
       [TearDown]
       public void TearDown()
       {
         if (File.Exists(RECIPE_FILE_NAME))
20       {
           File.Delete(RECIPE_FILE_NAME);
         }
       }

25     [Test]
       public void SaveAndRestore()
       {
         Recipe originalRecipe = new Recipe();
         originalRecipe.Name = CHEESEBURGER;
30       originalRecipe.AddIngredient(SIRLOIN);
         originalRecipe.AddIngredient(CHEESE);
         originalRecipe.AddIngredient(BACON);

         Stream recipeStream;
35       RecipeFile filer;
         using (recipeStream =
             File.OpenWrite(RECIPE_FILE_NAME))
         {
           filer = new RecipeFile();
40         filer.Save(recipeStream, originalRecipe);
         }

         // Now get it back
         Recipe reconstitutedRecipe;
45       using (recipeStream =
             File.OpenRead(RECIPE_FILE_NAME))
         {
           filer = new RecipeFile();
           reconstitutedRecipe = filer.Load(recipeStream);
50       }

         Assert.That(
           reconstitutedRecipe.Name,
           Is.EqualTo(originalRecipe.Name)
55       );

         int originalIngredientCount =
           originalRecipe.Ingredients.Count;
```

```
60      Assert.That(
          reconstitutedRecipe.Ingredients.Count,
          Is.EqualTo(originalIngredientCount)
        );

65      for (int i=0; i < originalIngredientCount; i++)
        {
          Assert.That(
            reconstitutedRecipe.Ingredients[i],
            Is.EqualTo(originalRecipe.Ingredients[i])
70        );
        }
      }
    }
```

RecipeTest.cs

At line 10, we'll declare some constant strings for testing. Then we make a new, empty object and populate it with the test data beginning at line 29. We could just pass literal strings directly into the object instead and not bother with const data members, but since we'll need to check the results against these strings, it makes sense to put them in common constants that we can reference from both spots.

With a Recipe data object now fully populated, we'll call the Save() method to write the recipe to disk at line 40. Now we can make a new Recipe object and ask the helper to load it from that same file at line 49.

With the restored object in hand, we can now proceed to run a whole bunch of asserts to make sure the test data we set in the originalRecipe object has been restored in the reconstitutedRecipe object.

Finally, we play the part of a good neighbor and delete the temporary file we used for the test in the TearDown method. As we mentioned in Chapter 3, the TearDown method will get executed to ensure that the file gets deleted, even if one of the assertions fails.

Now we can run the unit test in the usual fashion to make sure that the code is reading and writing to disk OK.

Try running this example before reading on...

STOP

```
Failures:
1) RecipeTest.SaveAndRestore:
   Expected string length 0 but was 12. Strings differ at index 0.
   Expected: "Cheeseburger"
   But was:  <string.Empty>
   -----------^
   at RecipeTest.SaveAndRestore() in RecipeTest.cs:52
```

Whoops! It seems that wasn't working as well as we thought—we're not getting the name line of the recipe back. When we save the file out in `RecipeFile.cs`, the code is using the key string `"NAME"` to identify the field, but when we read it back in (line 57 of `Load()`), it's trying to use the string `"TITLE"`. That's just not going to work. We can easily change that to read `"NAME"` to match the key used for the save, but stop and ask yourself this critical question:

Could this happen anywhere else in the code?

Using strings as keys is a fine idea, but it does open the door to introduce errors because of misspellings or inconsistent naming, as we've seen here. So perhaps this failing test is trying to tell us something more—perhaps we should refactor the code and pull out those literal strings into constants. The class then looks like this:

```
Line 1    public class RecipeFile
    -     {
    -         const string NAME_TOKEN = "NAME";
    -         const string INGREDIENTS_TOKEN = "INGREDIENTS";
    5
    -         public Recipe Load(Stream savedRecipe)
    -         {
    -             using (StreamReader reader = new StreamReader(savedRecipe))
    -             {
   10                 string line;
    -                 List<string> lines = new List<string>();
    -                 while ((line = reader.ReadLine()) != null)
    -                 {
    -                     lines.Add(line);
   15                 }
    -
    -                 return createRecipe(lines);
    -             }
    -
   20             return recipe;
    -         }
    -
    -         public void Save(Stream savedRecipe, Recipe recipe)
    -         {
   25             using (StreamWriter file =
    -                     new StreamWriter(savedRecipe))
    -             {
    -                 file.WriteLine(
```

```
  -          "{0}={1}",
30             NAME_TOKEN,
  -            recipe.Name
  -        );
  -
  -        file.WriteLine(
35           "{0}={1}",
  -          INGREDIENTS_TOKEN,
  -          recipe.Ingredients.Count
  -        );
  -        foreach (string line in recipe.Ingredients)
40
  -        {
  -          file.WriteLine(line);
  -        }
  -      }
  -    }
45   }
  -
  -   private Recipe createRecipe(ICollection<string> lines)
  -   {
  -     char[] delim = new char[] {'='};
50     Recipe recipe = new Recipe();
  -     foreach (string line in lines)
  -     {
  -       string[] tokens = line.Split(delim, 2);
  -
55       switch (tokens[0])
  -       {
  -         case NAME_TOKEN:
  -         {
  -           recipe.Name = tokens[1];
60           break;
  -         }
  -         case INGREDIENTS_TOKEN:
  -         {
  -           try
65           {
  -             int count = Int32.Parse(tokens[1]);
  -             for (int i = 0; i < count; i++)
  -             {
  -               recipe.AddIngredient(line);
70             }
  -           }
  -           catch (IOException error)
  -           {
  -             throw new RecipeFormatException(
75               "Bad ingredient count: " + error.Message);
  -           }
  -           break;
  -         }
  -       }
80     }
  -
  -     return recipe;
  -   }
  - }
```

RecipeFile.cs

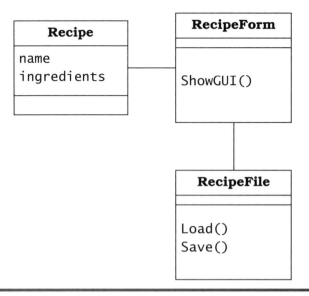

Figure 9.3: REFACTORED RECIPES STATIC CLASS DIAGRAM

We've improved the original program a lot with these simple changes. In order to test the file I/O, we did the following:

- We made Recipe a first-class object.

- We moved file I/O routines out of the GUI and into RecipeFile to narrow the class's responsibility.

- We pulled literals into constants to avoid bugs from typos and reduce duplication.

Finally, now that we have unit tests that provide the basic capabilities of a Recipe, we need to reintegrate the new Recipe class into the GUI itself and tend to the file I/O. We'd like to end up with something like Figure 9.3.

Now RecipeForm holds an object of type Recipe and uses the helper class RecipeFile to read and write recipes to disk. When the user clicks the Save button, the GUI will set values from the widgets in the Recipe object and call RecipeFile.Save(). When a new recipe is loaded in, the GUI will get the proper values from the Recipe object returned from RecipeFile.Load().

Testing a GUI can be very hard, but that's usually because the code is written in such a way as to make it difficult. This kind of code isn't uncommon either—this is what happens when you use the WinForms designer to generate code and then just integrate logic directly into the generated method's code. It can be tempting to use something like NUnitForms (covered in the next chapter) to test this kind of logic, but if we went that route, our tests would end up long and complicated.

By separating the pure GUI-related code from the actual logic of the application, we can easily add and test business features without having to worry about how we're going to weave the features into the GUI code.

The main GUI class `RecipeForm` (formerly known as `Recipes`) should now contain nothing but GUI-oriented code: widgets, callbacks, and so on. Thus, all the "business logic" and file I/O can be in non-GUI, fully testable classes.

And we've got a clean design as an added bonus.

We're not done with this code yet, but now it's your turn to make some modifications.

9.3 Testing the Class Invariant

Another way to improve the design of a class is by defining and verifying the "class invariant."[1]

A class invariant is an assertion, or some set of assertions, about objects of a class. For an object to be valid, all these assertions must be true. They cannot vary.

For instance, a class that implements a sorted list may have the invariant that its contents are in sorted order. That means no matter what else happens and no matter what methods are called, the list must always be in sorted order—at least as viewed from outside the object. Within a method, of course, the invariant may be momentarily violated as the class performs whatever housekeeping is necessary.

---

[1]For more information on preconditions, postconditions, and invariants, see [Mey97].

But by the time the method returns or the object is otherwise available for use (as in a multithreaded environment), the invariant must hold true, or else it indicates a bug. That means it's something you could check for as part of every unit test for this class.

The invariant is generally an artifact of implementation: internal counters, the fact that certain member variables are populated, and so on. The invariant is not the place to check for user input validation or anything of that sort. When writing tests, you want to test just your one thing, but at the same time you want to make sure the overall state of the class is consistent—you want to make sure you have not inflicted any collateral damage.

Here are some possible areas where class invariants might apply.

Structural

The most common invariants are structural in nature. That is, they refer to structural properties of data. For instance, in an order-entry system you might have invariants such as the following:

- Every line item must belong to an order.

- Every order must have one or more line items.

When working with arrays of data, you'll typically maintain a member variable that acts as an index into the array. The invariants on that index would include the following:

- The index must be $>= 0$.

- The index must be $<$ array length.

We want to check the invariant if any of these conditions are likely to break. Suppose we are performing some sort of calculation on the index into an array; we'd want to check the invariant throughout our unit tests to make sure the class is never in an inconsistent state. We showed this in the stack class example on page 79.

Structural errors will usually cause the program to throw an exception or terminate abruptly. For that matter, so will failing the invariant check. The difference is that when the invariant is violated, we know about it right away—right at the scene of the crime. We'll probably also know exactly what condition was violated. Without the invariant, the failure may occur far from the original bug, and backtracking to the cause might take you anywhere from a few minutes to a few *days*.

More important, checking the invariant makes sure we aren't passing the tests based just on luck. It may be that there's a bug that the tests aren't catching that will blow up under real conditions. The invariant might help us catch that early, even if an explicit test does not.

Mathematical

Other constraints are more mathematical in nature. Instead of verifying the physical nature of data structures, we may need to consider the logical model. For example:

- Debits and credits on a bank account match the balance.

- Amounts measured in different units match after conversion (an especially popular issue with spacecraft).

This starts to sound a lot like the boundary conditions we discussed earlier, and in a way they are. The difference is that an invariant must always be true for the entire visible state of a class. It's not just a fleeting condition; it's *always* true.

Data Consistency

Oftentimes an object may present the same data in different ways—a list of items in a shopping cart, the total amount of the sale, and the total number of items in the cart are closely related. From a list of items with details, we can derive the other two figures. It must be an invariant that these figures are consistent. If not, then there's a bug.

9.4 Test-Driven Design

Test-driven development is a valuable technique where you always write the tests themselves *before* writing the methods that they test [wCA04]. As a nice side benefit of this style of working, you can enjoy "test-driven design" and significantly improve the design of your interfaces.

You'll get better interfaces (or APIs) because you are "eating your own dog food," as the saying goes—you are able to apply feedback to improve the design.

That is, by writing the tests first, you have now placed yourself in the role of a *user* of your code, instead of the *implementor* of your code. From this perspective, you can usually get a much better sense of how an interface will really be used, and you might see opportunities to improve its design.

For example, suppose we're writing a routine that does some special formatting for printed pages. We need to specify a bunch of dimensions, so we code up the first version like this:

```
AddCropMarks(PSStream str, double paper_width,
                          double paper_height,
                          double body_width,
                          double body_height);
```

Then as we start to write the tests (based on real-world data), we notice that a pattern emerges from the test code:

```
public Process() {
    AddCropMarks(str, 8.5, 11.0, 6.0, 8.5);
    AddCropMarks(str, 8.5, 11.0, 6.0, 8.5);
    AddCropMarks(str, 8.5, 11.0, 6.0, 8.5);
    AddCropMarks(str, 5.0, 7.0, 4.0, 5.5);
    AddCropMarks(str, 5.0, 7.0, 4.0, 5.5);
}
```

As it turns out, there are only a handful of common paper sizes in use, but we still need to allow for oddball sizes as necessary. So, the first thing to do—just to make the tests easier, of course—is to factor out the size specification into a separate object:

```
PaperSpec standardPaper1 = new PaperSpec(8.5, 11.0,
                                         6.0, 8.5);
PaperSpec standardPaper2 = new PaperSpec(5.0, 7.0,
                                         4.0, 5.5);
XXX XX XXXXXXX XX   XX XXXX  X XXX XXX X XX XXX
XX X XXX XXXX XXX XX  XXX XXX XX X X X XX;
AddCropMarks(str, standardPaper1);
AddCropMarks(str, standardPaper1);
XX XXX XX X X XXX XX   XX XXX XX X XX XXX X;
XXX XX XXXXX XXX X XX X XX XXX XX XX X XXX;
AddCropMarks(str, standardPaper2);
```

Now the tests are much cleaner and easier to follow, and the application code that uses this will be cleaner as well.

Since these standard paper sizes don't vary, we can make a factory class that will encapsulate the creation of all the standard paper sizes:

```
public class StandardPaperFactory {
  public static PaperSpec LetterInstance;
  public static PaperSpec A4Instance;
  public static PaperSpec LegalInstance;
  XXXXX XXXXX XXXXXXXX X XXXXXXXXX;
  XXXXX XXXXX XXXXXXXX X XXXXXXXXX;
}
```

By making the tests cleaner and easier to write, we will make the real code cleaner and easier to write as well.

Try It

Exercises

7. Design an interest calculator that calculates the amount of interest based on the number of working days in between two dates. Use test-first design, and take it one step at a time.

Answer on 217

9.5 Testing Invalid Parameters

One question that comes up when folks first start testing is this: "Do I have to test whether my class validates its parameters?" The answer, in best consultant fashion, is "It depends. . . ."

Is your class supposed to validate its parameters? If so, then yes, you need to test that this functionality is correct. But there's a larger question here: "Who is responsible for validating input data?"

In many systems, the answer is mixed or haphazard at best. You can't really trust that any other part of the system has checked the input data, so you have to check it yourself—or at least, that aspect of the input data that particularly concerns you. In effect, the data ends up being checked by everyone and no one. Besides being a grotesque violation of the DRY principle [HT00], it wastes a lot of time and energy—and we typically don't have that much extra to waste.

In a well-designed system, you establish up front the parts of the system that need to perform validation and localize those to a small and well-known part of the system.

So, the first question we should ask about a system is, "Who is *supposed* to check the validity of input data?"

Generally we find the easiest rule to adopt is the "keep the barbarians out at the gate" approach. Check input at the boundaries of the system, and you won't have to duplicate those tests inside the system. Internal components can trust that if the data has made it this far into the system, then it must be OK.

It's sort of like a hospital operating room or industrial "clean room" approach. You undergo elaborate cleaning rituals before you—or any tools or materials—can enter the room, but once there, you are assured of a sterile field. If the field becomes contaminated, it's a major catastrophe; you have to re-sterilize the whole environment.

Any part of the software system that is outward-facing (a UI, or interface to another system) needs to be robust and not allow any incorrect or unvalidated data through.

What defines "correct" or valid data should be part of specification you're testing against.

What does any of this have to do with unit testing?

It makes a difference with regard to what you need to test against. As we mentioned earlier, if it isn't your code's responsibility to check for input data problems, then don't waste time checking for it. If it *is* your responsibility, then you need to be extra vigilant—because now the rest of the system is potentially relying on you, and you alone.

But that's OK. You've got unit tests.

Chapter 10

UI Testing

In the previous chapter, we successfully extracted core functionality that was intertwined with UI code. Now that we've separated the logic from our UI code, what is there left to test in the UI code? And how is this a "unit test" when the UI is involved?

10.1 Unit Testing WinForms

We're going to see how this works in the real world using the NUnitForms framework, which is an extension of NUnit (http://nunitforms.sourceforge.net). Alas, NUnitForms uses Win32 native calls to work its magic and therefore doesn't currently work under Mono. Because NUnitForms itself depends upon NUnit, you may find that the version of nunit.framework.dll you are referencing during compilation of our code isn't the same version as the one NUnitForms was built against. (The compiler will actually warn us of this.) Don't panic—we'll talk more about this later in the chapter.

Let's get started. There's no magic here; remember that unit tests are just code, and controls (forms included) are just objects. For instance, we can create and use additional constructors and not just be stuck with the default empty constructor. If a form requires a Recipe object to display, for example, then the form should have a constructor that takes a Recipe parameter.

Andy's Rant on GUI Testing

"Some people are convinced that they *must* compare bitmaps to do GUI testing. Well, that is simply the most antiquated, 1970s bit of thinking I can imagine. For crying out loud, I wrote a GUI tester based on X11 back in 1992 or so that was object-oriented (in other words, it worked with the OK button object on a form, and placement was irrelevant), was scriptable, could do live record and playback, and then later could do editing of the event, test composition, and so on. And that was some fifteen years ago."

Now we've got a first easy unit test that doesn't require NUnitForms—pass null in for the parameter, and expect an ArgumentNullException:

```
[TestFixture]
public class RecipeFormTest
{
  [Test]
  [ExpectedException(typeof(ArgumentNullException))]
  public void NullRecipe()
  {
    new RecipeForm(null);
  }
}
```

What can we test that's actually GUI-related? The RecipeForm has two buttons: Save and Cancel. You want to make sure the Save button calls the Save() method on the RecipeFile object that is passed to it. (We're concerned only with the GUI functionality of the Save button—the behavior of the RecipeFile.Save() method is tested elsewhere.) We'll use mock objects to make our lives easier:

```
using NUnit.Framework;
using NUnit.Framework.SyntaxHelpers;
using NUnit.Extensions.Forms;
using RecipeViewer;
using System;
```

```csharp
namespace RecipeViewer.Tests
{
  public class FakeRecipeFile : RecipeFile
  {
    UInt32 saveCalled = 0;
    public UInt32 SaveCalled
    {
      get { return saveCalled; }
    }
    public override Save()
    {
      saveCalled++;
    }
  }
  [TestFixture]
  public class RecipeFormTest
  {
    [Test]
    public void Save()
    {
      FakeRecipeFile recipe = new FakeRecipeFile();
      RecipeForm recipeForm =
        new RecipeForm(recipe as Recipe);
      recipeForm.Show();
      ButtonTester saveButton = new ButtonTester("Save");
      saveButton.Click();
      Assert.That(recipe.SaveCalled, Is.EqualTo(1));
    }
  }
}
```

First, we create a fake object for Recipe that tracks the number of calls to the Save() method. Then, we make a new RecipeForm and give it our FakeRecipe object, add the control to a form, and finally call the Show() method on the RecipeForm. When we run the test, the form with the control will pop up quickly (don't blink or you'll miss it).

Next, we create a ButtonTester for the Save button. Note that the ButtonTester isn't based on the contents of the button's Text property but rather the Name property. Make sure you give these sane names and not use the default ones generated by the designer.

We then call the Click() method on the ButtonTester and ask the fake Recipe how many times Save() was called. We want to assert that it was called only once.

Pretty cool, huh? By faking the model, we kept the unit test very focused even though it was testing the GUI. We could also use one of the mock object frameworks discussed in Chapter 6.

Here's another example we want to make sure works: clicking the Cancel button *doesn't* save the recipe:

```
[Test]
public void Cancel()
{
  FakeRecipe recipe = new FakeRecipe();
  RecipeForm recipeView =
    new RecipeForm(recipe as Recipe);
  Form form = new Form();
  form.Add(recipeView);
  form.Show();
  ButtonTester cancelButton = new ButtonTester("Cancel");
  cancelButton.Click();
  Assert.That(recipe.SaveCalled, Is.EqualTo(0));
}
```

We introduced a little duplication here with the previous test, so it's time to refactor a bit. First, extract `recipe` and `recipeView` to be class-level fields; then, extract the initialization of those fields into `SetUp()` so they're fresh for each test method. We've eliminated duplicate code, so we're ready to proceed.

Mocking the User

NUnitForms can also simulate a user changing fields in the GUI via the keyboard, and all other kinds of things, relatively easily. There's only one major exception, and that's modal dialogs:

```
[TestFixture]
public class LoginModalDialogTest : NUnitFormTest
{
  const string PASSWORD_FAILURE = "Password Failure";

  [Test]
  public void PasswordFailureClickOK()
  {
    ExpectModal(PASSWORD_FAILURE,
      "MessageBoxOkHandler");
    MessageBox.Show("Try again?", PASSWORD_FAILURE);
  }
```

```
public void MessageBoxOkHandler()
{
  MessageBoxTester messageBox =
    new MessageBoxTester(PASSWORD_FAILURE);

  Assert.That(
    messageBox.Title,
    Is.EqualTo(PASSWORD_FAILURE)
  );
  messageBox.ClickOk();
}
}
```

Modal dialogs are interesting because they suspend the program until they're dismissed. Thankfully, NUnitForms has a way to deal with that—by using the ExpectModal method in the NUnitFormTest class.

To use it (or any other NUnitForms methods), we derive our fixture from NUnitFormTest and call ExpectModal, passing the name of the caption (a.k.a. title) of the modal dialog. When a modal dialog is displayed that has the specified caption, the handler method is called. So in our handler method, we do our button clicks, assertions, and so on, and then we dismiss the dialog as a user would. Then our tests continue on their merry way.

10.2 Unit Testing Beyond Windows Forms

What if you're using a UI library that isn't Windows Forms? This isn't unthinkable, and it certainly isn't untestable either. There are some nuances, but many of the concepts presented thus far apply equally. You just won't have a nice framework like NUnitForms to help you along.

For other common GUI toolkits, such as Qt# and Gtk#, there is some variance in the ease of testing. Qt# is a .NET binding to the open source C++ native library, Qt. Qt 4.1 and newer has a built-in unit testing framework called QTestLib. Gtk# is also a wrapper (in essence), but neither the wrapper nor the native library has a unit testing framework associated with it as of the time of this writing.

> ### Testing Code That Runs on the GPU
>
> *Thanks to Ryan Dy, a programmer on some of Matt's favorite Xbox games for this real-world detail.*
>
> Sometimes there are transformations that aren't done on the CPU; they're done on the GPU via shader programs. In that case, you need to expose the shader variables to your test code running on the CPU, so you can assert against them in your tests. This is a common method for debugging shader code, and it also allows you to make sure your shader performs similarly across different hardware implementations in an automated fashion.

What about custom GUIs, like ones that are 3D?[1] That turns out to be easier in some cases—you have more control over improving the design and can make the GUI code easier to test.

Most 3D applications use a scene graph, such as a tree of nodes, where each node in the tree represents something to be drawn in the space. The nodes know their X, Y, and Z (distance from the camera) coordinates and their length along those planes. A visitor class[2] visits each node in the scene graph. The visitor class is responsible for tasks such as rendering the node in the 3D space or passing messages such as mouse clicks or keyboard interactions.

It's relatively straightforward to see where testing could be introduced in this common 3D scenario. First, we may want to test the nodes themselves, but they are usually data only—all the behavior generally goes into the visitor objects that apply transformations to the data contained in the nodes.

---

[1] For instance, a C# wrapper around OpenGL, such as Tao: see its website at http://www.taoframework.com.

[2] Fun fact: Scene graphs are one of the few places that the Visitor design pattern is commonly applied.

Next, we could test the scene graph and make sure its underlying tree is self-balancing (or whatever other behavior you expect). Last, the visitor classes themselves can be unit tested if they are well-encapsulated and loosely coupled with the rest of the design.

This is a lot of talk to be sure; how can we actually code up a test that makes sure that our layout algorithm fits all the nodes onto the rendered screen? We might sketch out a test that looks like this:

```
[Test]
public void NoNodesOutsideOfScreenBounds()
{
  Node[] nodes = createNodesOfVaryingLengths(1000);
  sceneGraph.Add(nodes);
  sceneGraph.Accept(new LayoutVisitor());
  Assert.That(anythingOutOfBounds(sceneGraph), Is.False);
}
```

We have a creation method to help us create the nodes for this test, which is ultimately data-driven. We load the scene-Graph with the test data, and then sceneGraph accepts the LayoutVisitor.

As mentioned previously, the Visitor pattern is often applied in applications that employ scene graphs. In this instance, we are testing the LayoutVisitor to make sure it doesn't place any of the nodes offscreen once it is finished.

You would probably test other visitors this way as well. What's this magical method called anyNodesAreOutOfBounds? It's sometimes easier to write the test as you'd like it to read and to then work backward and fill in the missing pieces.

Now that we have the test like we'd like it to read, here's the code for the aforementioned magical method. It is basically a simple software renderer whose sole purpose is to assist this particular kind of testing.

Note that RectangleF is a struct from the System.Drawing namespace.

```
private bool anythingOutOfBounds(SceneGraph sceneGraph)
{
  foreach(Node node in sceneGraph)
  {
    RectangleF rect = new RectangleF();
    rect.Width = node.MaxWidth * node.ZScale;
    rect.Height = node.MaxHeight * node.ZScale;
    rect.X = node.X * node.ZScale;
    rect.Y = node.Y * node.ZScale;
    if (rect.X >= MAX_DISPLAY_WIDTH)
    {
      return true;
    }
    if (rect.Bottom <= 0)
    {
      return true;
    }
  }
  return false;
}
```

One reviewer pointed out that this helper method could actually be encapsulated into a OutOfBoundsCheckVisitor object, which you could apply to the scene graph and then later query. This is a great idea to help keep the test code object-oriented, and we encourage you to apply the extract class refactoring [FBB+99] when appropriate—even in test code.

10.3 Web UIs

An entire book could be written about testing web-based UIs. We'll touch on the concept briefly here because many people are under the impression this is not possible or requires expensive commercial tools. First, many "Web 2.0" applications have a great deal of their functionality in JavaScript (a.k.a. ECMAScript). Unlike the dark ages of ten years ago, JavaScript is now an open ECMA standard with frameworks available that make object orientation and unit testing a snap. In many modern applications, much of the important end-user functionality is on the client side in JavaScript. The server-side code mostly accepts Ajax requests that either retrieve or store data in the database with some data validation and logging.

As such, unit testing the JavaScript is the first step. We recommend JsUnit,[3] which provides a framework and a test runner that can run within most modern browsers. You can assert that your JavaScript code is having the correct effect on specific DOM elements, such as adding or removing styles, child nodes, or whatever. This allows us to find and test for bugs that would otherwise have to be done manually with visual inspection.

We also recommend using a framework such as Prototype or JQuery that provides various syntactic and functional helpers that make JavaScript a little easier to code and test. All sorts of nifty Ajax libraries and frameworks are available, but you should make sure they don't hinder your ability to unit test functionality. See the JsUnit website for examples—you can apply many of the concepts from this book equally between C#, JavaScript, and other languages.

To test web applications beyond JavaScript and server-side objects, you can use a free, open source tool called Selenium.[4] With Selenium, you can write code that drives any of the mainstream browsers on the operating system of your choice. It works by running a server that launches a browser, which accepts commands via a socket and translates those commands into browser clicks and keyboard input.

This means we can write NUnit tests that look like this:

```
[Test]
public void AnchoviesNotAvailableInMontana()
{
  ISelenium selenium =
    new DefaultSelenium(
      "localhost", 4444, "firefox2",
      "http://localhost:56789/OrderPizza.aspx"
    );
  selenium.Select(INGREDIENT_DROPDOWN_ID, "anchovies");
  selenium.Type(STATE_TEXT_ID, "montana");
  selenium.Click("submit");
  selenium.WaitForCondition(
      "selenium.isTextPresent('Not Available')"
  );
}
```

---

[3]http://www.jsunit.net
[4]http://www.openqa.org/selenium/index.html

> \\\//
> ≥ƒ≤   Joe Asks...
> ~̃
> ### Aren't Selenium Tests More Like System Tests?
>
> Yes, Selenium tests aren't really unit tests, even though you are driving the browser in NUnit. ASP.NET doesn't have a good way to isolate the various handlers for testing or to do a lightweight integration test as of the time of this writing.[a] As such, you have to apply a holistic approach to get much of the same benefit. The ASP.NET pages and controls should be a thin layer on top of other, more easily testable objects—just like for WinForms or any other widget library. Selenium then helps us test the interaction between the web server configuration, web controls, and underlying objects. It is slower, mainly because of the overhead of starting and running a real browser, but it is definitely better than manual web UI testing. When using a system testing tool such as Selenium, make sure to exclude it from your code coverage measurements. Your unit tests alone should provide high levels of code coverage; measuring the coverage of system-level tests obscures that valuable feedback of unit-level test coverage.
>
> ---
>
> [a]WebWork and Rails do, which are Java- and Ruby-based, respectively.

We instantiate a new Selenium controller, which starts the Selenium server. This in turn starts the browser. We tell the Selenium controller to select "anchovies" from a list control. Note that the location and style of that control don't really matter—we're just working off the HTML IDs. Because we have stored the HTML IDs into a variable, we have to change them in only one place should the HTML ID in the user interface change. Then, we tell Selenium to type **montana** in the input control. Next, we tell Selenium to click a button with the HTML ID of "submit"; last, we wait for the validator (or whatever else) text to appear.

If the condition isn't met by the default timeout,[5] the test will fail. One interesting side note is that selenium.isTextPresent is a snippet of JavaScript that will tell Selenium what to do on the browser side.

Selenium tests are like any other tests; you tend to do the same things over and over. Being the pragmatic programmers that we are, we don't stand for duplication. When we see it, we refactor by extracting methods, extracting a class, and performing other refactorings.

A common pattern with Selenium is to wrap the Selenium instance and delegate to it. By doing this, you can have assertion and helper methods tied to a project-specific Selenium object that can be shared:

```
namespace PizzaWeb.Test.UI
{
  public class MySelenium
  {
    protected ISelenium selenium;
    public MySelenium(string host,
                      int port,
                      string[] browsers,
                      string url)
    {
      selenium =
        new DefaultSelenium(host, port, browsers, url);
    }
    public Stop()
    {
      selenium.Stop();
    }
    public void waitForText(string expectedText)
    {
      selenium.WaitForCondition(
        "selenium.isTextPresent('" + expectedText + "')"
      );
    }
  }
}
```

Something else that is often duplicated is the creation of the Selenium instance and the closing of the browser.

---

[5]This is sixty seconds in Selenium 0.9.

Another common pattern is to have a base class from which
other Selenium-oriented classes derive:

```
namespace PizzaWeb.Test.UI
{
  public abstract class MySeleniumFixture
  {
    static final uint SELENIUM_SERVER_PORT = 56789;
    protected MySelenium selenium;
    [TestFixtureSetUp]
    public void StartBrowser()
    {
      selenium = new MySelenium(
        "localhost", SELENIUM_SERVER_PORT,
        "firefox2", getInitialUrl()
      );
    }
    [TestFixtureTearDown]
    public void StopBrowser()
    {
      selenium.Stop();
    }

    protected abstract string getInitialUrl();
  }
  [TestFixture]
  public class OrderPizzaTest : MySeleniumFixture
  {
    static final string INGREDIENT_DROPDOWN_ID =
                                  "ingredients";
    static final string STATE_TEXT_ID = "state";
    string getInitialUrl()
    {
      return "http://localhost:7890/OrderPizza.aspx";
    }
    [Test]
    public void AnchoviesNotAvailableInMontana()
    {
      selenium.Select(
        INGREDIENT_DROPDOWN_ID,
        "anchovies"
      );
      selenium.Type(STATE_TEXT_ID, "montana");
      selenium.Click("submit");
      selenium.waitForText("Not Available");
    }
  }
}
```

When making the Selenium instance, only one thing generally varies from test to test: the initial URL the browser loads.
To reuse the creation of the Selenium instance, we extracted

it into a method and then into a base class from which the test fixture itself derives. We marked that creation method with the `TestFixtureSetUp` attribute, so we don't keep closing and opening the browser for every test. Your application may need to close the browser for each test, though, in which case we should use `SetUp` and `TearDown` instead. The base class defines the abstract method called `getInitialUrl()`, which the derived class must implement. When we add a new test fixture for a different web page, we'll override that method and get the benefits of reuse.

In our example we set the default browser to "firefox2." If you want to test with Opera or Internet Explorer as well, you can make sure your tests pass under both browsers by adding "IE6" or "opera" (respectively) to the third parameter of the `DefaultSelenium` constructor.

10.4 Programmer UIs

If you're creating a reusable library or framework, your API is the UI for your primary users—programmers like you. All of the UI unit testing concepts presented earlier still apply. Your public API methods should be a thin layer that delegates to other more easily testable objects. A good reason for this is because an API that might be easy to consume as a programmer won't necessarily be loosely coupled and easily testable [CA05]. If you can't introduce new public classes to your assembly because you have to match a documented specification,[6] you might be tempted to make the supporting classes behind your API facade internal. At that point, you would then have to compile your test code in the library's assembly itself so the unit tests could access those internal classes. There are various suboptimal (and downright ugly) ways to force this scenario, but we suggest extracting a separate assembly that contains the underlying support classes for your API. This way, your library's public API facade can remain spotless, and you can still easily unit test the underlying support classes.

---

[6]All .NET implementations, for instance, have to exactly match the public classes and methods specified by the ECMA-335 CLI standard.

In some cases, the .NET class libraries expose both a difficult to test but convenient to use API and an easier to test but more verbose version. This is what Microsoft recommends in its Framework Design Guidelines [CA05], and we agree.

10.5 Command-Line UIs

Before we finish talking about UI testing, we can't forget about our old friend the command line. Once again, the first step is to make sure our static `Main()` method is a thin layer that mostly interacts with other, more easily testable objects. Often, argument parsing is done in a quick and dirty fashion right in the `Main()` method. What do you do if there is a bug in the command-line argument parsing, and we want to write a unit test that fails when the bug is present and passes when it is fixed? Say we had code like this:

```
private static void isTracing;
public static void Main(string[] args)
{
  if (args.Length < 1)
  {
    printUsage();
    Environment.Exit(-1);
  }
  if (args[0] == "--trace")
  {
    isTracing = true;
  }
}
```

There is a bug (or lack of feature, depending on your personal outlook) where the `trace` command-line option is recognized only when it is the first argument. We want to unit test the change regardless because text processing is one of those areas in our experience where bugs tend to creep back in as seemingly "safe" changes are made. One way would be to write a test like this:

```
[Test]
public void TraceAsSecondArgument()
{
  TextUI.Main(new String[] {"filename", "--tracing"});
  Assert.That(Main.IsTracing, Is.True);
}
```

This test wouldn't compile as it is written—we would have to add a static property called `IsTracing` to our class. If you find yourself thinking this doesn't feel right, we would agree with you. Like the other UI testing paradigms we've discussed, we want `Main()` to be a thin layer that does a little coordination between other objects. Adding a property makes it fatter rather than thinner.

Instead, let's first extract a method that will help highlight some better seams along which we can extract a class that we can then unit test:

```
private static bool hasTracing(string[] args)
{
  return (args[0] == "--trace");
}
```

Now here's something we can unit test more easily. Testing the `Main()` class still feels a little weird, so let's extract that static method into a class called `Args`. Once we do that, we can write a test like this:

```
[Test]
public void TraceAsSecondArgument()
{
  Args args = new Args(
    new string[] {"filename", "--tracing"}
  );
  Assert.That(args.IsTracing, Is.True);
}
```

This example backs up Andy's rant from the beginning of the chapter. Unit testing most UI code is hard only because people *think* it is, not because it is actually technically challenging.

Once you just approach the problem as though it is solvable, it becomes one of the more trivial issues you'll deal with in your professional career.

10.6 GUI Testing Gotchas

GUI testing is fairly straightforward, save for a couple of gotchas that we'll discuss now. Don't be scared—knowing about these issues up front deflates their difficulty quite a bit.

Conflicting NUnit Libraries

If NUnitForms was built against a specific version of NUnit that differs from the version of the NUnit libraries you're referencing in your project, you'll get a compiler warning telling you as such. This usually doesn't present a problem, but if it does, there's an easy way to fix it.

Download the NUnitForms source code, and replace its NUnit libraries with the version of NUnit you're using. Then build NUnitForms, and store the custom build in your project's lib/ directory. This seems like a big deal, but it's a minor annoyance at worst. You'll have to rebuild when there's a new NUnitForms release that you *must* deploy, but that's about it.

Automated Build

There's a simple "gotcha" here worth mentioning when using NUnitForms (or similar tools) in an automated build.

If your automated build runs as a service, you will be unable to show any modal dialogs. Attempting to do so will result in an exception that basically says "Don't show modal dialogs in a service."

This is historical and does make some sense. Since the service doesn't have a desktop where someone could dismiss a modal dialog, the service would get stuck, and the machine would require a reboot. This happened enough times with poorly written commercial applications that Microsoft nipped it in the bud by disallowing it altogether.

There is an easy workaround, and it's only a little messy. Start your automated build controller from a logged-in account, via a batch file or shell script. Then set the build machine to log in on boot automatically and run the batch file on start-up for that user. It ends up practically the same as running the service, but you won't run into the aforementioned issue with modal dialogs.

Multithreaded and Complex Controls

Now it's time for a more advanced gotcha.

If you're testing a form that contains a control that is multithreaded and does interesting things with the Win32 event loop (such as MSHTML, the Internet Explorer HTML rendering control), you may find it doesn't work correctly when you try to unit test it. It might only partially draw its contents, not draw anything at all, or not respond to the input provided by NUnitForms. This is because the event loop doesn't work the same in this test runner as it does when running under regular Windows.

You can work around this by calling `Application.DoEvents()`, which will suspend your current thread and run the message pump thread until there are no pending Win32 events in the queue.

In the case of some unreasonably complex controls (for example, MSHTML), you may have to run `Application.DoEvents()` a couple of times in order for you to be able to coerce them into behaving as they would in the real world. How many times you need to call `Application.DoEvents()` will depend on the specific control and what your code is asking it to do. For instance, the MSHTML control may need more event loop flushes if it is rendering a document that loads images versus rendering a simpler document.

You can definitely unit test most GUIs, but be careful, because it's easy to end up writing system tests instead of unit tests. Testing only at the system level can sometimes seem much easier because you work around the need to refactor the code to make it more testable. Don't fall into that trap. As we've said a couple of times, one of the biggest values of unit testing is in making your designs better. On top of that, many unit-level tests can usually run in the same amount of time as a single system-level test.

Don't sell yourself, or your project, short by taking the easier way out. Be mindful of the balance between unit-level tests and system-level tests.

Appendix A

Gotchas

Here are some popular *gotchas*, that is, issues, problems, or misconceptions that have popped up over and over again to trap the unwary.

A.1 As Long As the Code Works

Some folks seem to think that it's OK to live with broken unit tests as long as the code itself works. Code without tests—or code with broken tests—*is* broken. You just don't know where or when. In this case, you've really got the worst of both worlds: all that effort writing tests in the first place is wasted, and you still have no confidence that the code is doing what it ought to be doing.

Note that a test that has *no* assert statements or (mock object verification) will count as "passed." This is arguably a bug in NUnit, but at any rate a test without asserts still counts as broken.

If the tests are broken, treat them just as if the code were broken.

A.2 Smoke Tests

Some developers believe that a *smoke test* is good enough for unit testing. That is, if a method makes it all the way to the end without blowing up, then it passed.

You can readily identify this sort of a test; there are no asserts within the test itself, just one big `Assert.IsTrue(true)` at the end. Maybe the slightly more adventurous will have multiple `Assert.IsTrue(true)` throughout, but no more than that. All they are testing is, "Did it make it this far?"

And that's just not enough. Without validating any data or other behavior, all you're doing is lulling yourself into a false sense of security—you might think the code is tested, but it is not.

Watch out for this style of testing, and correct it as soon as possible. *Real testing checks results.* Anything else is just wasting everyone's time.

A.3 "Works on My Machine"

Another pathological problem that turns up on some projects is that old excuse "It's not broken; it works on my machine." This points to a bug that has some correlation with the environment. When this happens, ask yourself the following:

- Is everything under version control?

- Is the development environment consistent on the affected machines?

- Is it a genuine bug that just happens to manifest itself on another machine (because it's faster, has more or less memory, and so on)?

End users, in particular, don't like to hear that the code works on *your* machine and not theirs.

All tests must pass on *all* machines; otherwise, the code is broken.

A.4 Floating-Point Problems

Quite a few developers appear to have missed that one day in class when they talked about floating-point numbers. It's a fact of life that there are floating-point numbers that can be only approximately represented in computer hardware.

The computer has only so many bits to work with, so something has to give.

This means 1.333 + 1.333 isn't going to equal 2.666 exactly. It will be close but not exact. That's why the NUnit floating-point asserts require you to specify a *tolerance* along with the desired values (see the discussion on page 34).

But still you need to be aware that "close enough" may be deceptive at times. Your tests may be too lenient for the real world's requirements, for instance. Or you might puzzle at an error message that says this:

```
Failures:
1) TestXyz.TestMe :
       expected:<1.00000000>
        but was:<1.00000000>
  at TestXyz.TestMe() in TestXyz.cs:line 10
```

"Gosh, they sure look equal to me!" But they aren't—there must be a difference that's smaller than is being displayed by the print method.

As a side note, you can get a similar problem when using date and time types. Two dates might look equal as they are normally displayed—but maybe the milliseconds aren't equal.

A.5 Tests Take Too Long

Unit tests need to run fairly quickly. After all, you'll be running them a lot. But suddenly you might notice that the tests are taking *too long*. It's slowing you down as you write tests and code during the day.

That means it's time to go through and look at your tests with a fresh eye. Cull out individual tests that take longer than average to run, and group them using the [Category] attribute discussed on page 45.

You can run these optional, longer-running tests once a day with the build or when you check in, but not have to run them every single time you change code.

Just don't move them so far out of the way that they *never* get run.

A.6   Tests Keep Breaking

Some teams notice that the tests keep breaking over and over again. Small changes to the code base suddenly break tests all over the place, and it takes a remarkable amount of effort to get everything working again.

This is usually a sign of excessive coupling. Test code might be too tightly coupled to external data, to other parts of the system, and so on. Remember that a singleton is really just a global variable wearing pretty clothes—if other bits of code can muck with its state, they will, usually when you least expect it.

As soon as you identify this as a problem, you need to fix it. Isolate the necessary parts of the system to make the tests more robust by using the same techniques you would use to minimize coupling in production code. See [HT00] for more details on orthogonality and coupling or [FBB+99] for information on refactoring and "code smells." And don't forget to use mock objects (Chapter 6) to decouple yourself from the real world.

A.7   Tests Fail on Some Machines

Here's a common nightmare scenario: all the tests run fine—on most machines. But on certain machines they fail consistently. Maybe on some machines they even fail intermittently.

What on Earth could be happening? What could be different on these certain machines?

The obvious answer is differences in the version of the operating system, the libraries, the C# runtime engine, the database driver—that sort of thing. Different versions of software have different bugs, workarounds, and features, so it's quite possible machines configured differently might behave differently.

But what if the machines are configured with identical software, and you still get different results?

It might be that one machine runs a little faster than the other, and the difference in timing reveals a race condition or other problem with concurrency. The same thing can show up on single- versus multiple-processor machines.

It's a real bug; it just happened not to have shown up before. Track it down on the affected machine using the usual methods. Prove the bug exists *on that machine* as best you can, figure out a way to make the existing test (or a new one) fail more consistently, and verify that all tests pass *on all machines* when you are done.

A.8 Tests Pass in One Test Runner, Not the Other

You may find a situation where all the tests pass for you using `nunit-gui`, the GUI test runner, but fail in the automated build, which uses `nunit-console`. This can be an indicator of hidden global state, circular object dependencies, or `Finalizer` bugs.

That last one can be especially subtle. For instance, there was a case where the developer wrote their finalizer like it was a C++ destructor—they were accessing the object's fields. But in the .NET environment, the fields may be garbage collected before the `Finalizer` is executed. The result? An intermittent `NullReferenceException`. In this case, it happened only in the `nunit-console` test runner when launched from NAnt via CruiseControl.NET, aligning the stars of the garbage collection universe just so. But once diagnosed, it also explained seemingly random crashes that can't be reproduced in the field as well.[1]

More likely, `nunit-console` and other test runners can run tests in slightly different order, which may expose hidden dependencies.

---

[1]For more on garbage collection "gotchas," see [Sub05].

A.9 Thread State Issues

Sometimes we see strange `InvalidOperationException`, `ThreadStateException`, or COM-based exceptions get thrown when code runs under NUnit, but not in production. This can sometimes be related to the apartment-type being multithreaded when it should be single-threaded, and vice versa. These are usually referred to by the acronyms MTA and STA, respectively. This is deep .NET voodoo we don't want to get stuck in, but there are a couple of NUnit command-line options to try: `-thread` and `-domain`. See the NUnit documentation for more information on these options. If you have a burning desire to learn more, a quick perusal through CLR via C#[Ric06] or a web search will give you more information.

A.10 C# 2.0–Specific Issues

So far, we haven't mentioned too many things specific to C# 2.0, so how do we use NUnit on a project that uses C# 2.0? We do just as we normally would, with a couple of minor exceptions.

First we'll need to use a version of NUnit that is compiled with a C# 2.0 compiler. There are separate packages on the NUnit website for .NET 1.1 and 2.0 versions. By the way, it's perfectly safe and OK to use the .NET 2.0–compiled NUnit on a C# 1.1 project; the developers will just have to have .NET 2.0 or Mono 1.1 or newer installed to run the tests.

Another notable thing to watch out for is the interaction of `Assert.IsNull()` and `Assert.IsNotNull()` with Nullable types. Nullable types, a C# 2.0 feature, allows value types such as int, `DateTime`, enums, or structs to have a "null" value when it is not initialized. This feature was added so that the language could map more closely to the way databases represent data (for more information, see [Ric06]).

If we write a test like this, then it will fail:

```
[Test]
public void NullableInt() {
  int? first;
  Nullable<int> second;

  Assert.IsNull(first);
  Assert.IsNull(second);
}
```

The reason why is because the value isn't literally null. The first line and second lines of code are semantically identical; the question mark syntax is just some syntactic sugar to make it easier to consume in C#. Looking at the second declaration, we can see it is a struct of type Nullable<T>. This will never be null.

To correctly test whether the Nullable type has a value, check its HasValue property:

```
Assert.IsTrue(first.HasValue)
```

Appendix B

Resources

B.1 On the Web

CruiseControl.NET
⇒ `http://ccnet.thoughtworks.com`
CruiseControl.NET is an automated continuous integration server for .NET that integrates with NAnt, NUnit, NCover, and most major open source and proprietary version control systems.

DotGNU
⇒ `http://dotgnu.org`
DotGNU is an open source implementation of the ECMA standards upon which C# and .NET are based. It sports C# and .NET 1.1 support as well an optimizing JIT compiler as of this writing. It is not as complete as Mono, another open source implementation.

DotNetMock
⇒ `http://sourceforge.net/projects/dotnetmock`
This is a repository for mock object information in the .NET environment, as well as for testing in general.

Mono
⇒ `http://mono-project.com`
This is another open source implementation of the ECMA standards upon which C# and .NET are based. It supports C# and .NET 2.0 as well as an optimizing JIT compiler.

NAnt
⇒ `http://nant.sourceforge.net`
A popular cross-platform build system for compiling, testing, packaging, and deploying, based upon Ant for Java. It has easy

integration for NUnit, NCover, NCoverExplorer, FxCop, and Visual Studio solution and project files. Most automated build systems use NAnt to do the majority of the heavy lifting.

NCover
⇒ http://ncover.org

NCover is a simple code coverage tool that runs from the command line and outputs an XML file with the code coverage statistics. It requires debug information for monitored assemblies and produces line-by-line visit counts. It also includes a simple XSLT transform to make the output readable in a browser.

NCoverExplorer
⇒ http://kiwidude.com/blog

This is a WinForms GUI and command-line UI for summarizing and exploring the XML files that NCover emits. It also includes NAnt tasks, style sheets, and tasks for CruiseControl.NET. It allows for failure of a build if code coverage gathered during the build and test are below a certain watermark.

NMock2
⇒ http://nmock.org

NMock is a dynamic mock object library for .NET.

NUnit
⇒ http://nunit.org

This xUnit-based unit testing tool for Microsoft .NET is written entirely in C# and has been completely redesigned to take advantage of many .NET language features, including custom attributes and other reflection-related capabilities. NUnit brings xUnit to all .NET languages.

Pragmatic Programming
⇒ http://www.pragmaticprogrammer.com

This is the home page for the Pragmatic Programmers and your authors. Here you'll find all of the source code examples from this book, additional resources, updated URLs and errata, and news on additional volumes in this series and other resources.

SharpDevelop
⇒ http://www.sharpdevelop.net

This is a fully featured and stable open source IDE for .NET development. It has tight integration with NAnt, NUnit, NCover, code analysis, and source control.

TestDriven.NET
⇒ http://www.testdriven.net

This offers Visual Studio integration for NUnit and NCover. It works with the Express versions of Visual Studio, unlike other add-on products.

xUnit
⇒ http://www.xprogramming.com/software.htm

This provides unit testing frameworks for many, many different languages and environments.

B.2 Bibliography

[CA05]   Krzysztof Cwalina and Brad Abrams. *Framework Design Guidelines: Conventions, Idioms, and Patterns for Reusable .NET Libraries.* Addison Wesley Longman, Reading, MA, 2005.

[Cla04]   Mike Clark. *Pragmatic Project Automation. How to Build, Deploy, and Monitor Java Applications.* The Pragmatic Programmers, LLC, Raleigh, NC, and Dallas, TX, 2004.

[FBB⁺99]   Martin Fowler, Kent Beck, John Brant, William Opdyke, and Don Roberts. *Refactoring: Improving the Design of Existing Code.* Addison Wesley Longman, Reading, MA, 1999.

[Fea04]   Michael Feathers. *Working Effectively with Legacy Code.* Prentice Hall, Englewood Cliffs, NJ, 2004.

[Fow03]   Martin Fowler. *Patterns of Enterprise Application Architecture.* Addison Wesley Longman, Reading, MA, 2003.

[HT00]   Andrew Hunt and David Thomas. *The Pragmatic Programmer: From Journeyman to Master.* Addison-Wesley, Reading, MA, 2000.

[Mey97]   Bertrand Meyer. *Object-Oriented Software Construction.* Prentice Hall, Englewood Cliffs, NJ, second edition, 1997.

[MFC01]   Tim Mackinnon, Steve Freeman, and Philip Craig. Endo-testing: Unit testing with mock objects. In Giancarlo Succi and Michele Marchesi, editors, *Extreme Programming Examined*, chapter 17, pages 287–302. Addison Wesley Longman, Reading, MA, 2001.

[Pug06]   Ken Pugh. *Interface Oriented Design.* The Pragmatic Programmers, LLC, Raleigh, NC, and Dallas, TX, 2006.

[Ric06]   Jeffrey Richter. *CLR via C#.* Microsoft Press, Redmond, WA, second edition, 2006.

[SH06]   Venkat Subramaniam and Andy Hunt. *Practices of an Agile Developer: Working in the Real World*. The Pragmatic Programmers, LLC, Raleigh, NC, and Dallas, TX, 2006.

[Sub05]   Venkat Subramaniam. *.NET Gotchas*. O'Reilly & Associates, Inc, Sebastopol, CA, 2005.

[TH03]   David Thomas and Andrew Hunt. *Pragmatic Version Control Using CVS*. The Pragmatic Programmers, LLC, Raleigh, NC, and Dallas, TX, 2003.

[wCA04]   Kent Beck with Cynthia Andres. *Extreme Programming Explained: Embrace Change*. Addison-Wesley, Reading, MA, second edition, 2004.

Pragmatic Unit Testing: Summary

General Principles

- ☐ Test anything that might break.
- ☐ Test everything that does break.
- ☐ New code is guilty until proven innocent.
- ☐ Write at least as much test code as production code.
- ☐ Run local tests with each compile.
- ☐ Run all tests before check-in to the repository.

Questions to Ask

- ☐ If the code ran correctly, how would I know?
- ☐ How am I going to test this?
- ☐ What *else* can go wrong?
- ☐ Could this same kind of problem happen anywhere else?

What to Test: Use Your "Right BICEP"

- ☐ Are the results **right**?
- ☐ Are all the **b**oundary conditions CORRECT?
- ☐ Can you check **i**nverse relationships?
- ☐ Can you **c**ross-check results using other means?
- ☐ Can you force **e**rror conditions to happen?
- ☐ Are **p**erformance characteristics within bounds?

Good Tests Are "A TRIP"

- ☐ **A**utomatic
- ☐ **T**horough
- ☐ **R**epeatable
- ☐ **I**ndependent
- ☐ **P**rofessional

CORRECT Boundary Conditions

- ☐ **C**onformance: Does the value conform to an expected format?
- ☐ **O**rdering: Is the set of values ordered or unordered as appropriate?
- ☐ **R**ange: Is the value within reasonable minimum and maximum values?
- ☐ **R**eference: Does the code reference anything external that isn't under direct control of the code itself?
- ☐ **E**xistence: Does the value exist (for example, is non-null, non-zero, present in a set, and so on)?
- ☐ **C**ardinality: Are there exactly enough values?
- ☐ **T**ime (absolute and relative): Is everything happening in order? At the right time? In time?

Answers to Exercises

Exercise 1: *from page 89*

A simple stack class. Push String objects onto the stack, and Pop them off according to normal stack semantics. This class provides the following methods:

```
using System;

public interface StackExercise {
    /// <summary>
    /// Return and remove the most recent item from
    /// the top of the  stack.
    /// </summary>
    /// <exception cref="StackEmptyException">
    /// Throws exception if the stack is empty.
    /// </exception>
    String Pop();

    /// <summary>
    /// Add an item to the top of the stack.
    /// </summary>
    /// <param name="item">A String to push
    /// on the stack</param>
    void Push(String item);

    /// <summary>
    /// Return but do not remove the most recent
    /// item from the top of the stack.
    /// </summary>
    /// <exception cref="StackEmptyException">
    /// Throws exception if the stack is empty.
    /// </exception>
    String Top();

    /// <summary>
    /// Returns true if the stack is empty.
```

```
        /// </summary>
        bool IsEmpty();
    }
```

Here are some hints to get you started: What is likely to break? How should the stack behave when it is first initialized? How should it behave after it has been used for a while? Does it really do what it claims to do?

Answer 1:

- For a new stack, `IsEmpty()` should be `true`, and `Top()` and `Pop()` should throw exceptions.

- Starting with an empty stack, call `Push()` to push a test string onto the stack. Verify that `Top()` returns that string several times in a row and that `IsEmpty()` returns `false`.

- Call `Pop()` to remove the test string, and verify that it is the same string.[1] `IsEmpty()` should now be true. Call `Pop()` again verify an exception is thrown.

- Now do the same test again, but this time add multiple items to the stack. Make sure you get the right ones back, in the right order (the most recent item added should be the one returned).

- Push a `null` onto the stack and `Pop` it; confirm you get a `null` back.

- Ensure you can use the stack after it has thrown exceptions.

Exercise 2:   *from page 89*
A shopping cart. This class lets you add, delete, and count the items in a shopping cart.

What sort of boundary conditions might come up? Are there any implicit restrictions on what you can delete? Are there any interesting issues if the cart is empty?

```
public interface ShoppingCart {
    /// <summary>
    /// Add this many of this item to the
    /// shopping cart.
    /// </summary>
    /// <exception cref="ArgumentOutOfRangeException">
    /// </exception>
```

---

[1] In this case, the `Is.EqualTo()` constraint isn't good enough; you need `Is.Same()` to ensure it's the same object.

```
void AddItems(Item anItem, int quantity);
/// <summary>
/// Delete this many of this item from the
/// shopping cart
/// </summary>
/// <exception cref="ArgumentOutOfRangeException">
/// </exception>
/// <exception cref="NoSuchItemException">
/// </exception>
void DeleteItems(Item anItem, int quantity);
/// <summary>
/// Count of all items in the cart
/// (that is, all items x qty each)
/// </summary>
int ItemCount { get; }

/// Return iterator of all items
IEnumerable GetEnumerator();
}
```

ShoppingCart.cs

Answer 2:

- Call `AddItems` with a quantity of 0, and `ItemCount` should remain the same.

- Call `DeleteItem` with a quantity of 0, and `ItemCount` should remain the same.

- Call `AddItems` with a negative quantity, and it should raise an exception.

- Call `DeleteItem` with a negative quantity, and it should raise an exception.

- Call `AddItems`, and the item count should increase, whether the item exists already or not.

- Call `DeleteItem` where the item doesn't exist, and it should raise an exception.

- Call `DeleteItem` when there are no items in the cart, and `ItemCount` should remain at 0.

- Call `DeleteItem` where the quantity is larger than the number of those items in the cart, and it should raise an exception.

- Call `GetEnumerator` when there are no items in the cart, and it should return an empty iterator (in other words, it's a real IEnumerable object—not null—that contains no items).

- Call `AddItem` several times for a couple of items, and verify that contents of the cart match what was added (as reported via `GetEnumerator()` and `ItemCount()`).

Hint: You can combine several of these asserts into a single test. For instance, you might start with an empty cart, add three of an item, and then delete one of them at a time.

Exercise 3: *from page 90*

A fax scheduler. This code will send faxes from a specified filename to a U.S. phone number. There is a validation requirement; a U.S. phone number with area code must be of the form *xnn-nnn-nnnn*, where *x* must be a digit in the range [2..9] and *n* can be [0..9]. The following blocks are reserved and are not currently valid area codes: *x*11, *x*9*n*, 37*n*, 96*n*.

The method's signature is as follows:

```
///
/// Send the named file as a fax to the
/// given phone number.
/// <exception cref="MissingOrBadFileException">
/// </exception>
/// <exception cref="PhoneFormatException">
/// </exception>
/// <exception cref="PhoneAreaCodeException">
/// </exception>
public bool SendFax(String phone, String filename)
```

Given these requirements, what tests for boundary conditions can you think of?

Answer 3:

- Phone numbers with an area code of 111, 211, up to 911, 290, 291, ..., 999, 370–379, or 960–969 should throw a Phone-AreaCodeException.

- A phone number with too many digits (in one of each set of number, area code, prefix, number) should throw a PhoneFormatException.

- A phone number with not enough digits (in one of each set) should throw a PhoneFormatException.

- A phone number with illegal characters (spaces, letters, and so on) should throw a PhoneFormatException.

- A phone number that's missing dashes should throw a Phone-FormatException.

- A phone number with multiple dashes should throw a Phone-FormatException.

- A null phone number should throw a PhoneFormatException.

- A file that doesn't exist should throw a MissingOrBadFile-Exception.

- A null filename should also throw that exception.

- An empty file should throw a `MissingOrBadFileException`.

- A file that's not in the correct format should throw a `Missing-OrBadFileException`.

Exercise 4: *from page 90*

An automatic sewing machine that does embroidery. The class that controls it takes a few basic commands. The coordinates (0,0) represent the lower-left corner of the machine. *x* and *y* increase as you move toward the upper-right corner, whose coordinates are x = `TableSize.Width` - 1 and y = `TableSize.Height` - 1.

Coordinates are specified in fractions of centimeters.

```
public void MoveTo(double x, double y);
public void SewTo(double x, double y);
public void SetWorkpieceSize(double width,
                             double height);
public Size WorkpieceSize { get; }
public Size TableSize { get; }
```

Some real-world constraints might be interesting: you can't sew thin air, of course, and you can't sew a workpiece bigger than the machine.

Given these requirements, what boundary conditions can you think of?

Answer 4:

- Huge value for one or both coordinates

- Huge value for workpiece size

- Zero or negative value for one or both coordinates

- Zero or negative value for workpiece size

- Coordinates that move off the workpiece

- Workpiece bigger than the table

Exercise 5: *from page 91*

Audio/video-editing transport. A class that provides methods to control a DVD or media player. There's the notion of a "current position" that lies somewhere between the beginning (historically, BOT for "beginning of tape") and the end (EOT).

You can ask for the current position and move from there to another given position. *Fast-forward* moves from current position toward the

EOT by some amount. *Rewind* moves from current position toward the BOT by some amount. When media is first loaded, it is positioned at BOT automatically.

```
using System;
public interface AVTransport {
  /// Move the current position ahead by this many
  /// seconds. Fast-forwarding past EOT
  /// leaves the position at EOT
  void FastForward(double seconds);

  /// Move the current position backwards by this
  /// many seconds. Rewinding past zero leaves
  /// the position at zero
  void Rewind(double seconds);

  /// Return current time position in seconds
  double CurrentTimePosition();

  /// Mark the current time position with label
  void MarkTimePosition(String name);

  /// Change the current position to the one
  /// associated with the marked name
  void GotoMark(String name);
}
```

AVTransport.cs

Answer 5:

- Verify that the initial position is the BOT.

- Fast-forward by some allowed amount (not past EOT), and then rewind by same amount. You should be at the initial location.

- Rewind by some allowed amount (not before BOT), and then fast-forward by the same amount. You should be at the initial location.

- Fast-forward past EOT, and then rewind by the same amount. You should be before the initial location by an appropriate amount to reflect that you can't advance the location past EOT.

- Try the same thing in the other direction (rewind past BOT).

- Mark various positions, and return to them after moving the current position around.

- Mark a position and return to it *without* moving in between.

Exercise 6:   *from page 92*
Audio/video-editing transport, Release 2.0. This is the same as earlier, but now you can position in seconds, minutes, or frames (there are exactly 30 frames per second in this example), and you can move relative to the beginning or the end.

Answer 6: Cross-check results using different units: move in one unit, and verify your position using another unit; move forward in one unit and back in another, and so on.

Exercise 7: *from page 173*
Design an interest calculator that calculates the amount of interest based on the number of working days in between two dates. Use test-first design, and take it one step at a time.

Answer 7: Here's a possible scenario of steps you might take. There is no right answer; this exercise is simply to get you to think about test-first design:

1. Begin by simply calculating the days between any two dates first. The tests might include the following:
   - Use the same value for first date and last date.
   - Try the normal case where first date < last date.
   - Try the error case where first date > last date.
   - Try dates that span a year boundary (from October 1, 2003, to March 1, 2004, for instance).
   - Try dates more than a year apart (from October 1, 2003, to December 1, 2006).

2. Next, exclude weekends from the calculation using the same sorts of tests.

3. Now exclude public and/or corporate holidays. This raises the potentially interesting question of how to specify holidays. You had to face that issue when writing the tests; do you think doing so improved the interface?

4. Finally, perform the interest calculation itself. You might start off with tests such as these:
   - The interest amount should never be negative (an invariant).
   - The interest when first date equals last date should be 0.0.

Index

Pragmatic advice for this career...

Pragmatic Thinking and Learning

Software development happens in your head. Not in an editor, IDE, or design tool. In this book by Pragmatic Programmer Andy Hunt, you'll learn how our brains are wired, and how to take advantage of your brain's architecture. You'll master new tricks and tips to learn more, faster, and retain more of what you learn.

- Use the Dreyfus Model of Skill Acquisition to become more expert • Leverage the architecture of the brain to strengthen different thinking modes • Avoid common "known bugs" in your mind • Learn more deliberately and more effectively • Manage knowledge more efficiently

Pragmatic Thinking and Learning:
Refactor your Wetware
Andy Hunt
(288 pages) ISBN: 978-1-9343560-5-0. $34.95
http://pragprog.com/titles/ahptl

Pomodoro Technique Illustrated

Do you ever look at the clock and wonder where the day went? You spent all this time at work and didn't come close to getting everything done. Tomorrow, try something new. In *Pomodoro Technique Illustrated*, Staffan Nöteberg shows you how to organize your work to accomplish more in less time. There's no need for expensive software or fancy planners. You can get started with nothing more than a piece of paper, a pencil, and a kitchen timer.

Pomodoro Technique Illustrated: The Easy Way to Do More in Less Time
Staffan Nöteberg
(144 pages) ISBN: 9781934356500. $24.95
http://pragprog.com/titles/snfocus

Land the Tech Job You Love

You've got the technical chops—the skills to get a great job doing what you love. Now it's time to get down to the business of planning your job search, focusing your time and attention on the job leads that matter, and interviewing to wow your boss-to-be.

You'll learn how to find the job you want that fits you and your employer. You'll uncover the hidden jobs that never make it into the classifieds or Monster. You'll start making and maintaining the connections that will drive your future career moves.

You'll land the tech job you love.

Land the Tech Job You Love
Andy Lester
(225 pages) ISBN: 978-1934356-26-5. $23.95
http://pragprog.com/titles/algh

The Passionate Programmer

This book is about creating a remarkable career in software development. Remarkable careers don't come by chance. They require thought, intention, action, and a willingness to change course when you've made mistakes. Most of us have been stumbling around letting our careers take us where they may. It's time to take control.

This revised and updated second edition lays out a strategy for planning and creating a radically successful life in software development *(the first edition was released as My Job Went to India: 52 Ways To Save Your Job)*.

The Passionate Programmer: Creating a Remarkable Career in Software Development
Chad Fowler
(200 pages) ISBN: 978-1934356-34-0. $23.95
http://pragprog.com/titles/cfcar2

Competitive Edge

Debug It!

Debug It! will equip you with the tools, techniques, and approaches to help you tackle any bug with confidence. These secrets of professional debugging illuminate every stage of the bug life cycle, from constructing software that makes debugging easy; through bug detection, reproduction, and diagnosis; to rolling out your eventual fix. Learn better debugging whether you're writing Java or assembly language, targeting servers or embedded micro- controllers, or using agile or traditional approaches.

Debug It! Find, Repair, and Prevent Bugs in Your Code
Paul Butcher
(232 pages) ISBN: 9781934356289. $34.95
http://pragprog.com/titles/pbdp

Practices of an Agile Developer

Agility is all about using feedback to respond to change. Learn how to • apply the principles of agility throughout the software development process • establish and maintain an agile working environment • deliver what users really want • use personal agile techniques for better coding and debugging • use effective collaborative techniques for better teamwork • move to an agile approach

Practices of an Agile Developer:
Working in the Real World
Venkat Subramaniam and Andy Hunt
(189 pages) ISBN: 0-9745140-8-X. $29.95
http://pragprog.com/titles/pad

Cutting Edge

The Definitive ANTLR Reference

This book is the essential reference guide to ANTLR
v3, the most powerful, easy-to-use parser generator
built to date. Learn all about its amazing new LL(*)
parsing technology, tree construction facilities,
StringTemplate code generation template engine,
and sophisticated ANTLRWorks GUI development
environment. Learn to use ANTLR directly from its
author!

**The Definitive ANTLR Reference: Building
Domain-Specific Languages**
Terence Parr
(384 pages) ISBN: 0-9787392-5-6. $36.95
http://pragprog.com/titles/tpantlr

Release It!

Whether it's in Java, .NET, or Ruby on Rails,
getting your application ready to ship is only half
the battle. Did you design your system to survive a
sudden rush of visitors from Digg or Slashdot? Or
an influx of real-world customers from 100
different countries? Are you ready for a world filled
with flaky networks, tangled databases, and
impatient users?

If you're a developer and don't want to be on call at
3 a.m. for the rest of your life, this book will help.

**Release It! Design and Deploy Production-Ready
Software**
Michael T. Nygard
(368 pages) ISBN: 0-9787392-1-3. $34.95
http://pragprog.com/titles/mnee

Pragmatic Starter Kit

Version control. **Unit Testing**. **Project Automation**. Three great titles, one objective. To get you up to speed with the essentials for successful project development. Keep your source under control, your bugs in check, and your process repeatable with these three concise, readable books from The Pragmatic Bookshelf.

Visit Us Online

Unit Testing in C# Home Page

http://pragprog.com/titles/utc2
Source code from this book, errata, and other resources. Come give us feedback, too!

Register for Updates

http://pragprog.com/updates
Be notified when updates and new books become available.

Join the Community

http://pragprog.com/community
Read our weblogs, join our online discussions, participate in our mailing list, interact with our wiki, and benefit from the experience of other Pragmatic Programmers.

New and Noteworthy

http://pragprog.com/news
Check out the latest pragmatic developments in the news.

Save on the PDF

Save over on the PDF version of this book. Owning the paper version of this book entitles you to purchase the PDF version at a great discount. The PDF is great for carrying around on your laptop. It's hyperlinked, has color, and is fully searchable. Buy it now at `pragmaticprogrammer.com/coupon`

Contact Us

Phone Orders:	1-800-699-PROG (+1 919 847 3884)
Online Orders:	`www.pragmaticprogrammer.com/catalog`
Customer Service:	`orders@pragmaticprogrammer.com`
Non-English Versions:	`translations@pragmaticprogrammer.com`
Pragmatic Teaching:	`academic@pragmaticprogrammer.com`
Author Proposals:	`proposals@pragmaticprogrammer.com`